The Unavailable Father

The Unavailable Father

Seven Ways Women Can Understand,
Heal, and Cope with a Broken
Father-Daughter Relationship

Sarah Simms Rosenthal, PhD

JOSSEY-BASS
A Wiley Imprint
www.josseybass.com

Published by Jossey-Bass
A Wiley Imprint
989 Market Street, San Francisco, CA 94103-1741—www.josseybass.com

Jossey-Bass books and products are available through most bookstores. To contact Jossey-Bass directly call our Customer Care Department within the U.S. at 800-956-7739, outside the U.S. at 317-572-3986, or fax 317-572-4002.

Jossey-Bass also publishes its books in a variety of electronic formats. Some content that appears in print may not be available in electronic books.

Library of Congress Cataloging-in-Publication Data

Rosenthal, Sarah Simms, 1956-
   The unavailable father : seven ways women can understand, heal, and cope with a broken father-daughter relationship / by Sarah Simms Rosenthal. — 1st ed.
       p. cm.
       Includes bibliographical references and index.
       ISBN 978-0-470-61414-3 (pbk.)
       1. Fathers and daughters. 2. Dysfunctional families. 3. Fathers—Psychology.
   4. Daughters—Psychology. I. Title.
   HQ755.85.R6597 2010
   155.9'24—dc22   2010006358

Printed in the United States of America
FIRST EDITION
PB Printing   10 9 8 7 6 5 4 3 2

Contents

To the memory of my beloved mother, Renee,
whose love saved me; and to my husband, Mitch,
with whom I found the freedom to write this book.

Acknowledgments

On a beach one day, I mentioned the idea for this book to my dear friend Alexandra Penney. She encouraged me from the beginning, and had my back the whole time. My thanks to her are immeasurable.

My agent, Laura Yorke, believed in this project from the beginning. My gratitude to her is immense.

Many thanks to the editor, Lara Asher, who has been gentle and kind and patient throughout the writing of this book.

Additional big thanks to Alan Rinzler for taking this project, improving it, and publishing it in an expeditious manner, while maintaining its integrity.

Two colleagues contributed their research, organizational, and editing skills: Susan Carey Dooley offered help, insight, and soulfulness through the early stages of this project and Jim Twaite added his consummate professionalism to this book and other projects.

Many thanks to Burt Fischler for his enormous contribution in getting my Web site up and running and for his remarkable creative acumen.

My sister-in-law Jane and brother-in-law Jack have fed me, literally and figuratively, and have given me laughs and love that I cherish over many years.

My brothers, Hank and Adam, though they had remarkably different experiences with my father, supported me in this effort.

Profuse thanks to all the wonderful women who agreed to be interviewed for this book, sharing their intimate lives with me and others. I am deeply appreciative of your generosity.

I want to thank my friends who enrich my life in myriad ways—I am blessed to have such caring and close friends. They are truly a gift.

I would be remiss if I didn't thank a few friends who played pivotal roles in bringing this book to fruition:

Annette Tapert, a stalwart supporter and friend, generously gave her time and energy and helped to put out fires; Joe Armstrong provided marketing ideas and many years of laughs and friendship; Shirley Lord gave unqualified support and constancy from the beginning; Lisa and Richard Plepler have been my cheerleaders in this effort, and have provided stellar ideas. I'm proud to call you family, as well as friends.

My mother is no longer with me, but her love rescued me and gave me sustenance. I miss her and think of her every day and hold her in my heart.

My devoted and loving husband, and best friend, Mitch, who has supported me unfailingly during the writing of this book, as he always has.

Introduction

This book is about and for women who grew up with "unavailable" fathers. These fathers come in many forms, but they all have a common characteristic: they failed to provide their daughters with the unconditional love and the feeling of security that a child requires to become a woman with a positive self-concept and the ability to form close adult relationships.

My interest in the lives of women who had unavailable fathers began with my own childhood and my relationship with my father. He was physically present but emotionally distant and even abusive toward me, though he behaved quite normally toward my brothers. My interest in this area grew over the course of my thirty-year career as a psychotherapist, during which I have worked with many women of all ages who have experienced problems with adult psychosocial adjustment that are related directly to a failed father-daughter relationship. When I decided to write this book, I supplemented my personal experience and the lessons I learned in my clinical practice by carrying out a large number of interviews with a diverse group of women.

My Father

I grew up in White Plains, New York, in what looked like the perfect suburban family. My mother was pretty—tall with thick black hair and brown eyes. My father was very handsome, five nine or ten, straight nose, wide-set green eyes, and black hair (at least until he got older and it turned gray). He was an announcer for CBS and worked odd hours, but a couple of nights a week, he'd be home in time for the family dinner. I was the middle child; I had one older and one younger brother, and to complete the picture, there was Jekyll, our much-loved family dog.

It all sounds so normal: my wonderful and loving mother; my successful father; my little brother and me huddled together on the stairs, trying not to get caught and sent to bed when we stayed up late to spy on one of our parents' parties. On the surface, it was a rerun of *Father Knows Best,* but what I remember most is the tension. The good nights were the ones when my father didn't come home. When he did, I held my breath from the time I heard his car door slam until he entered the house. I never knew what to expect.

If he was in a good mood, he'd be witty and funny. Everything would be okay. When he was in a bad mood, his rage dominated dinner, running so deep it took over the room. He behaved normally with my brothers. He wasn't a super-involved father, and he never played sports with them, but he didn't have the same anger toward them that he showed toward me. When he bothered to say something to me, it was always sarcastic. My two best friends were so afraid of him that when I invited them over, they'd ask if my father was there. If I said yes, they'd make an excuse about why they couldn't come.

I don't remember him ever tucking me in at night or reading me a bedtime story. I don't remember him hugging me or touching me. I felt his rejection so strongly that when I helped my mother fold laundry and his undershorts wound up in the pile in front of me, I'd throw them at my mother. If he wasn't going to touch me, I was certainly not going to touch something as intimate as his underwear.

Once when my mother and father and I were in the kitchen, my father turned to my mother and said, "We should have had one more child. It would have been a girl, and she would have had blonde hair and blue eyes." I have dark hair and dark eyes and was much too self-willed for my father. He was making sure that I knew that there was a daughter he might have loved. The daughter they never had.

I still feel that hurt. When I see a young girl on a beach or at a playground, swimming, throwing a ball, running with a father who has taken the time to be part of her life, I experience that deep yearning and hunger for the father who was never my champion or protector.

I do not know why my father distanced himself from me and treated me with derision. How could I? I was never close enough to him that he shared any thoughts or feelings that he may have had regarding his own childhood. I know only that his father was genial but unsuccessful, and that my father had worked very hard to rise above the poor socioeconomic class into which he had been born. I also know that he was exceedingly concerned with his appearance and with presenting an appropriate public image. I know too that he led a double life for many years, supporting my mother and his children in the suburbs while maintaining a mistress in New York City.

I do know that the hunger I experienced as a result of the failure to develop a relationship with my father led me to become obsessed with men. The first time was in eighth grade when I fell in love with my teacher. He was going through a divorce—his wife was having an affair with one of his friends—and the shock and humiliation of that had left him feeling depressed and insecure. Being adored, even by a thirteen year old, must have been a balm to him.

I stayed after class as often as I could, and we talked about the things that mattered to each of us. By the next year, when I was in ninth grade, the other students had begun to whisper that he and I were having an affair. We were not, but the rumors had their effect. My father who had heard the whispers, was angry, the principal was concerned about the possible repercussions, and I was forbidden to see my former teacher or even go into his classroom. It was a painful time for me: I had finally found someone who cared, and then the connection was severed.

You'd think my parents would have seen my intense attachment to my teacher as an indication that something was wrong. Maybe my mother did, but my father's anger overrode her. My father hated that teacher. He never understood why I'd been drawn to him, and he never let it go. The mention of the man's name even fifteen years later would cause him to explode. But this teacher wasn't a predator or a monster. He was sensitive, warm, and caring. I could talk to him. I doubt that my father knew why he hated the man so much. Perhaps he resented the fact that this teacher could have a close and meaningful relationship with me, as he himself could not. Or perhaps my father had some unresolved sexual feelings toward me and this teacher represented a threat on an unconscious level. The latter possibility might explain why my father went in the opposite direction with respect to physical contact with me: he never touched me, never even said a flattering word. But the truth is that I really cannot explain his extreme hatred for my teacher-confidant, anymore than I can explain why he never sought a close relationship with me.

When I had my first real love in the eleventh grade, my father went ballistic. I am Jewish, and the boy was Irish Catholic and lived on what my father considered the wrong side of the tracks. My father wouldn't speak to me for days after he learned of this relationship. When my father passed me on the stairs in the house, he didn't say a word, though there was no missing his rage when he looked at me. I continued to date this boy until I went away to college, and my poor mother was caught in the middle, trying to be a bridge between the wayward daughter and the furious father.

It never worked. My father continued to express his disapproval by ignoring me. I recognize now that my father's sexual possessiveness with respect to me would seem to suggest a strong, if twisted, attachment. I cannot explain this. The predominant feeling that I have with respect to my father is that of loss for the close, loving relationship that we never had.

As I grew older, I found myself involved in a couple of seriously damaging sadomasochistic relationships—heavily charged situations that I can see, in retrospect, were recreating the same explosive atmosphere I'd grown up with. My father had a visceral dislike of all my boyfriends. It was even worse when I married. I suspect my father was threatened and envious of my husband, who was confident and competent in a way my father was not. Even after my mother died, and I really tried to be kind to my father, he made it impossible to be with him and my husband in the same room.

Forgiveness is not an easy place to get to, but the alternative is to carry anger and resentment through life. This is very harmful for one's mental and physical well-being. It took many years for me to let it go, but I think it's a worthy goal. Which isn't to say that everyone has to have a relationship with one's father if it is too toxic to do so.

After my father died, I discovered that he had carried on a life-long affair with another woman. I contacted the woman, and though she was reluctant to do so, she finally agreed to meet me. I learned that his mistress had been a beautiful showgirl who had been a dancer at Radio City Music Hall in New York for many years, and I learned that she worshipped the ground my father walked on.

My father's mistress explained to me that their relationship did not develop because my father didn't love my mother. She assured me that my father had loved my mother very much. But he had loved her as well. The shock I felt after that meeting led me to deeply examine my relationship with my father and his attitude toward me. I wondered if my father's rage rose from anguish—at loving two women and hurting them both, at betraying the man he had meant to be. Maybe—and perhaps this is far-fetched—he was too honorable to allow his anger to scorch my mother, whom he had betrayed, and too needy to risk alienating the mistress he loved. Instead he directed it at me, his strong-willed daughter. Perhaps I filled the role of a woman in waiting whom he could punish for his flaws.

Seeing my father from a different perspective after meeting with his mistress, I gained some insight into my own reactions to his behavior toward me. In particular, I realized the past was drawing me into abusive relationships. Following this realization, I was able to make a different and happier choice. My husband, Mitch, is a nurturing man who has helped me to heal. For years I found it impossible to be without a man in my life; to be alone was to be in the abyss. Marriage has released me from the prison of such fear. Oddly, should I lose him now, I would feel free to be alone. I don't mean to make it sound like marriage is the answer to an unavailable father. That would be facile and untrue. Sometimes when one problem is solved, another pops up when the time is right. There are various routes to compensate and grow from the loss, though one can never completely make up for the past.

Given my relationship with my father, it is not surprising that I would wind up working as a therapist. Many therapists are consciously or unconsciously motivated to choose a career that will help them understand better their own experience and issues. During my career as a therapist, I have worked with a wide range of individuals in terms of age, gender, and socioeconomic status. However, many of my patients have been women who are around the same age as me, fifty-three, and many of these women have been quite successful professionally. From these women I have learned that the phenomenon of the unavailable father is very common among women in my generation. In part, this was the result of prevailing social attitudes.

The Father-Daughter Relationship in My Generation

To a generation of young girls who grew up in the era when Daddy went to work and Mom stayed home, one role model pointed in a different direction: girl detective Nancy Drew. "Since the death of her mother many years before," wrote author Edward Stretemeyer, "she had lived with her father, Carson Drew, a noted lawyer engaged largely in mystery cases. . . . Carson Drew was proud of his daughter and openly boasted that she had a talent for unearthing mysteries and solving baffling cases."

Carson Drew represented the ideal dad. Young girls curled up on the couch with a Nancy Drew mystery envied the young detective not only for her sporty blue roadster, but for her life with a father who encouraged her exploits. Cared for by a housekeeper who offered motherly ministrations without motherly interference and a father who adored her, Nancy was the envy of many young girls who found it hard to gain their father's attention, much less his approval.

The fact is, among women of my generation, fathers were much more likely to be involved with their sons than with their daughters. This norm was reflected not only in the popular culture but also in academic and professional circles. During my clinical training and in discussions with colleagues, I was made keenly aware of the importance of the mother-daughter relationship and the father-son relationship as templates for the development of the adult personality. In contrast, I rarely heard a therapist discuss the importance of the father-daughter relationship.

The prevailing consensus was that fathers and daughters tend not to have particularly close relationships, and that is okay. After all, fathers have traditionally been more likely to share interests with their sons than with their daughters, and shared interests tend to lead to more frequent contact, as well as to the bonds that develop when fathers experience and express their empathic understanding of the joys and the disappointments associated with participation in their sons' sports competitions, outdoor activities, and budding heterosexual social relationships.

In the course of my practice, I have certainly observed many fathers who attributed the successful developmental efforts of their sons to their own mentorship. Fathers often think of their sons as "chips off the old block." They derive significant gratification from the belief that they have had a substantial positive role in fostering their sons' mastery of the world and the challenges of growing up. The gratification associated with the assumption of the mentoring role is so rewarding for many men that it makes them even fonder of their sons, who come to represent living examples of their paternal expertise. I have heard many fathers state explicitly that they are much more important to their sons than to their daughters.

In contrast, many fathers seem willing to delegate the task of providing role models for daughters to their wives. They don't spend as much time with their daughters as they do with their sons. They don't talk to their daughters as much as they talk with their sons. They don't get to know their daughters as well as they get to know their sons. They tend not to view themselves as primarily responsible for their daughters' personal successes and accomplishments (although they may well attribute their daughters' good looks to their family genes).

As one might expect given the frequent occurrence of these long-standing attitudes of fathers regarding daughters, I have also encountered in my practice a large number of female patients who have complained explicitly about the lack of time they were able to spend with their fathers while they were growing up, as well as the failure of their fathers to encourage the development of close, meaningful relationships. A number of these patients stated explicitly that their fathers were simply unavailable to them physically and emotionally.

Some other female patients did not spontaneously bring up their disappointment with their relationships with their fathers, but only because they assumed that the norm is for fathers to remain aloof from their daughters. The women in this group never expected to be close to their fathers.

Yet some women with whom I have worked did have close relationships with their fathers while they were growing up, and these women often maintain these close relationships into adulthood. I have found that these women tend to feel better about themselves than women with weak paternal relationships. I have also found that women who have had close relationships with their fathers tend to be more successful academically and professionally than their counterparts with weaker paternal relationships. Those with close relationships with their fathers also appear to me to be generally more likely to be appropriately assertive and independent, and they are far less likely to become involved in self-destructive or acting-out behavior.

Social Change and the Contemporary Father-Daughter Relationship

Social changes that have occurred over the past several decades have tended to reduce somewhat the tendency of fathers to distance themselves from their daughters. Young girls more commonly become involved in competitive sports and other activities with which their fathers can identify, and it has become more acceptable for men to show their softer side. These changes allow fathers to be involved with and nurturing toward their daughters to a greater extent than was previously considered to be appropriate or normative.

Although there have been good and bad fathers in every generation and in every culture, it does appear that a higher proportion of today's fathers resemble Carson Drew. My younger friends and my younger female clients tend to report that their children's fathers constitute a new breed of caretaker. These young fathers are more likely to be highly involved in their children's lives in general and their daughters' lives in particular. They attend school functions, take their children for checkups, get to know their children's friends, and share experiences.

Among women in my generation, the norm was the strong mother-daughter bond and the weak father-daughter bond. And for women who are now painfully aware of how weak their relationships with their fathers have been, the involved younger fathers they observe today can serve as a painful reminder of what they have missed.

I believe the widespread social acceptance of the notion that fathers are not normally very close to their daughters goes a long way toward explaining why so many of my female clients have described their fathers as "distant" or "unavailable."

Over time, as I became more aware of the impact of the failed father-daughter relationship, I began to talk about it with many different women. The questions I asked inevitably sparked immediate interest and fascinating conversations. Though I live in New York, I have traveled widely and have been lucky enough to meet women in many different occupations and professions. I have found that many of the women I met have been interested in discussing their childhood years and the role their fathers had played or, sadly, had not played. Most had never discussed this topic with anyone, at least not in any detail. But they seemed anxious to do so.

By discussing the father-daughter relationship with many women from diverse backgrounds, I learned that fathers in any generation may be unavailable to their daughters for a variety of reasons that go far beyond the accepted social norms of the time period in which the relationship developed or failed to develop.

For many women, a failed father-daughter relationship is not the result of a cultural norm that says it is okay for fathers not to be close to their daughters, but rather the result of an identifiable issue or problem that is specific to the individual father. Perhaps he was the kind of man who had difficulties forming any close emotional bonds—a man who could not show love. Perhaps he had a mental illness or a substance abuse problem that rendered his behavior unpredictable, embarrassing, or anxiety producing. Perhaps he was an angry, impulsive individual who was verbally, physically, or even sexually abusive. Maybe he was simply a self-centered man who indulged his own needs and appetites while ignoring his responsibilities as a father. Finally, some fathers were unavailable to their daughters because they were simply absent. Some fathers die when their daughters are young children or adolescents. Some fathers pick up and leave.

The Impact of the Unavailable Father

Although fathers may be unavailable to form a close, loving relationship with their daughters for a variety of reasons, the failure of any father to form such a relationship with his daughter tends to have predictable consequences. Psychologists tell us that developing children require two important conditions to grow up feeling good about themselves and comfortable in their relationships to others: love and security.

The first of these conditions is often referred to as unconditional love. When a father makes it clear to his daughter in every way that he loves her unconditionally, just for who she is, he lays the foundation for her positive self-concept. When he conveys his approval for how she looks or the activities she pursues, he validates her existence. He helps her to become confident, self-assured, and ready to face the world.

The second of these two conditions is security. A daughter must feel that the world is predictable and significant others are dependable. She must be taught that her needs can be met. If a daughter is made to feel that she cannot depend on her parents to make certain that her needs are met, she will be likely to develop a pervasive general sense of apprehension and anxiety regarding the future. She may grow up to be a person who is always waiting for the rug to be pulled out from under her. She may hesitate to act on her own behalf, because she fears she might "upset the apple cart." And she may hesitate to trust others because she has learned that they cannot be trusted.

Young girls with unavailable fathers do not understand social norms that may discourage close father-daughter relationships, and they certainly do not understand the withholding behavior of a father who distances himself from his daughter because of his own neurotic conflicts, psychiatric diagnosis, or narcissistic selfishness. Therefore, young girls who experience disinterest, rejection, or abuse on the part of their fathers are likely to assume that his behavior is the result of some flaw within themselves.

I have observed consistently in my practice that the failure of the father-daughter relationship, whether due to neglect or abuse, can send a young girl into adulthood convinced she is a woman without worth, doomed to repeat professionally and personally the failure she felt with her father.

Yet some women overcome a childhood with an unavailable father. These women develop a sense of self-esteem despite the lack of paternal validation, and they build a successful life. These women may judge their success by the money they earn, the power they wield, or the personal happiness they've found. Each of these women has a lesson to teach all of us who lacked a father's recognition and love. Those lessons and the painful experiences and triumphs that led to them are the subject of this book.

The Archetypes

Based on my practice and my interviews with women, I have identified six types of fathers who are unavailable to their daughters, either because they do not communicate unconditional love or do not make their daughters feel secure and safe. I describe these types of fathers in the next six chapters, using the stories these daughters told me. You will find that some of the fathers fit quite snugly into one or another type, and others exhibit traits from more than one group.

Not many of the men set out to deliberately harm their daughters. Most, as their daughters came to learn, were not even aware of the harm they were inflicting. In many cases they were passing on the failures of their own parents, ensuring that the pain of the frightened child would pass on to yet another generation. In many cases, as was the case with my own relationship with my father, the issue of what aspects of their own childhood led these fathers to become unavailable remains unclear to the daughters, even after these daughters have become adults and have themselves wrestled with the fallout of their fathers' failures.

Throughout history, storytelling has been a way to form community. By confiding the details of a tragedy, the person who endured it rubs away the rawness; each time the story is repeated, the burden grows lighter. But each of the listeners now owns a part of that story and carries it for the victim. What the listener gets for sharing the burden is the assurance that bad things strike us all.

Those events are not a sign of our unworthiness or guilt. The storyteller has made each of us aware that we are all human, susceptible to the harsh blessing that Aeschylus described when he wrote, "Even in our sleep, pain which cannot forget falls drop by drop upon the heart, until, in our own despair, against our will, comes wisdom through the awful grace of God."

I hope the wisdom contained in these stories will reach out to other women who grew up feeling that their fathers did not love them. I hope these stories will allow such women to attain a perspective on their childhood relationships that will enable them to cast off the feelings of worthlessness and overcome the aching need for validation.

Most of the women interviewed shared their entire stories, and I have endeavored here to convey these stories largely in their own words. In this way, readers can see the setting in which the girl grew up, the dynamics of the family, and sometimes what the girl herself failed to see: her father really did care, although he was unable to show it. In a few of the interviews, I have followed the more usual procedure—letting quotations from their stories buttress the information I gleaned from others.

What has been changed are the names of the women and details that would make them easy to identify. Frankness can come with a price, and the price could be the destruction of father-daughter relationships they have worked hard to establish. What has not been changed are the stories they told me of the various ways fathers can damage daughters (and, of course, the way they can make them whole).

If you had an unavailable father, you will recognize yourself in one or another of these tales. In all of them, you will be given part of the burden carried by the storyteller and, I hope, wisdom to know that it was through no fault of her own that her father never really nurtured or supported her.

In Part Two of this book, I provide you with questions that you can ask yourself to determine whether your father fits into one of these categories of unavailable fathers, and I provide suggestions for steps that you can take to help you overcome the legacy of his unavailability and move on toward a better, more hopeful future.

Part One

Part One

The Stories

Chapter One

The Disapproving Father

One of the most frequently occurring themes that emerges from my interviews, clinical work, and personal experience is that of the disapproving father: the father who failed to provide his daughter with the type of unconditional love and approval that children require in order to develop a positive self-concept and a sense of personal self-efficacy on which they can rely in their interactions with the world. These women reported that for one reason or another, their fathers failed to validate their existence and their intrinsic worth as human beings.

In some cases, the father's disapproval and his failure to validate his daughter's existence and worth resulted from active antipathy for her, such as may occur when the father wanted a son instead, and he feels that he can relate only to a boy's interests and activities. Such a father may simply ignore his daughter's accomplishments, leaving her to wonder what is wrong with her.

Alternatively, the father may fail to show love for his daughter and praise her accomplishments because he is emotionally disconnected and doesn't feel pride in her achievements. He may be too preoccupied with his work, or he may be the narcissistic sort who cannot think of anyone's needs or accomplishments save his own.

In still other cases, the disapproving father is not disconnected at all. In fact, he is well aware of his daughter's achievements. However, he may praise her only when she achieves his view of perfection. He will not love her and communicate her value to him simply because she is his daughter. Instead, he makes her feel that only her accomplishments matter. Furthermore, the father who makes positive expressions of his daughter's worth contingent on her accomplishments may also set extremely high standards for approving these accomplishments. He may see the A that she earned in physics and ask her why she did not earn an A+.

All of these are disapproving fathers, and their failure to make their daughters feel valued unconditionally leads their daughters to assume that they are inadequate. These daughters often respond by redoubling their efforts to succeed in all areas of life in order to win the love and recognition that they require in order to feel good about themselves. This phenomenon explains why most of the women described in this chapter are remarkably successful by any objective criteria for success.

Unfortunately, it is often the case that nothing these women could ever accomplish during their formative years or even later would succeed in winning their father's approval. In the face of a consistent lack of love and approval, these daughters grow up feeling inadequate, often in the face of clear objective evidence to the contrary.

The stories that follow illustrate several different types of disapproving, invalidating fathers and the impact of their failure on the development of their daughters. They also provide us with an important clue regarding the means through which these women eventually gained self-acceptance and a feeling or personal worth. Time and again we find that when fathers fail to impart to their daughters a sense of personal worth, the daughters will seek out and secure validation through subsequent interaction with other significant individuals in their lives.

"If Only I Had Been a Boy"

Billie's father, Dan, clearly wanted a son. When his wife became pregnant, he went out and bought a large quantity of sports equipment and picked out the name William, the same name as his own father, whom he idolized. When a daughter arrived, Dan did his best to hide his disappointment and put the best face possible on the situation. He said they could name the daughter Billie with an "ie" at the end, and he could still play sports with her. He assumed she would be an athlete and maybe a bit of a tomboy. But it didn't work out that way. Billie was not particularly athletic, and she was all girl. She much preferred dolls and frilly dresses to footballs and blue jeans.

As it became more and more clear to Dan that Billie was 100 percent little girl, he felt increasingly uncomfortable around her. He didn't know how to relate to a child that he couldn't push around, wrestle with, and slap on the back. In reality, Dan made little effort to learn how he might relate to a girl, and he left the job of raising Billie to her mom. When his subsequent children were boys, Dan stopped relating to Billie at all. Billie became keenly aware that her younger brothers got a great deal of attention from her dad, while she got none.

But Billie didn't stop trying to measure up and gain his approval. When she reached school age, she assumed that if she couldn't impress her father with her athletic prowess, then perhaps she could impress him by being a perfect student. As her younger brothers reached school age as well, Billie realized that through hard work, she could make school the arena in which she could surpass their achievements. She excelled in all academic work. Perhaps because her father was an electrical engineer, she made a special effort to do particularly well in math and science.

Yet Billie's prodigious academic efforts brought little recognition from her father. He gave her perfect report cards little more than a compulsory nod, then turned to his sons to heap praise on their athletic accomplishments. He attended all the boys' games and took them camping, but he never attended the school assemblies at which Billie received so many awards. On the same day that he missed her grade school graduation (it occurred during his workday hours), he attended his youngest son's Little League game (which required him to leave work a half-hour early).

As Billie grew up, her father's failure to make her feel loved and valued led her to doubt her worth. Although she was very attractive, she was socially insecure. She was particularly uncertain of her attractiveness to men. She dated infrequently in high school and never had a steady boyfriend. She just focused on her studies.

As Billie neared graduation from high school, Dan made it quite clear to her that he would be able to provide only a modest amount of financial assistance for her college education. He had only one salary, and there were three children to put through college. Furthermore, he told her flat-out that "it was certainly more important for a boy to have a good college education than it was for a girl."

Although Billie had considered becoming a premedical student and was admitted to a prestigious private liberal arts college, she ultimately opted to attend the nearest branch of the state university, where she studied nursing. The idea of nursing also appealed to her because she thought of the nursing profession as a vehicle through which she could implement her nurturing impulses. Billie continued to excel in her studies. She graduated from nursing school ranked number one in her class, and she went on to a career as a neurosurgical intensive care nurse.

Once Billie began nursing school, her self-concept began to improve by leaps and bounds. There she received so many compliments from her professors and her fellow students that she finally began to think of herself as someone worthwhile. She also blossomed socially, discovering that many men in the college community sought her company because they found her physically and intellectually attractive.

After Billie started to work in the intensive care unit (ICU), her competence on the job and her excellent evaluations and promotions further boosted her self-concept. Eventually she mustered up the courage to apply to a doctoral program in nursing, and she was admitted with full financial support. She became the head nurse in the ICU, then the director of nursing at the hospital where the ICU was located.

In one of her graduate school courses, Billie met John, a doctoral student in psychology who loved everything about Billie— including her looks, her intellect, and her nurturing personality.

John was very demonstrative, and she flourished under the attention that he lavished on her. They got married, and today Billie is a confident, competent woman who loves her life and values the contributions that she makes to the world.

Billie's story illustrates the key problem experienced by women whose fathers fail to provide them with the unconditional love and validation that children require in order to develop a healthy self-concept. These women tend to overcompensate, often becoming high achievers, yet they typically fail to give themselves credit for their innate worth or accomplishments. Despite their successes, these women are often unsure of themselves.

Daughters of disapproving dads cannot think well of themselves and function well socially until they receive validation from some other source. Billie was fortunate in that the nursing education she pursued provided her with the validation that her father failed to provide, and over time she began to believe that she was a desirable individual. Once she felt that she had some intrinsic value, she could allow herself to interact with the world as both a giver and a receiver. When John told her that he loved her, she could believe him. She ended up happy, but she owes no thanks to her dad for her happiness.

Not all daughters of disapproving fathers have been so fortunate.

"He Never Showed Me He Cared"

Some fathers seem to be incapable of giving their daughters the affection and unconditional approval they must have to develop healthy, positive self-concepts. In these instances, there is virtually nothing that a daughter can do to get her father's attention and approval. Unfortunately, a developing child has no idea that the problem lies not with her but with her father's inability to bond. A young girl with a disconnected father is likely to assume that there must be something wrong with her to merit such treatment, and this assumption inevitably influences the manner in which she interacts with others. This dynamic of paternal disconnection is illustrated by Elizabeth.

Elizabeth is a thirty-nine-year-old vice president for catalogue design at the headquarters of a large sports store in the Midwest. She is married to a partner in a Minneapolis law firm. She has no children. Although she is attractive and successful, Elizabeth does not think of herself in these terms.

Elizabeth is truly a beauty. She's blonde, blue-eyed, tall, slender, and gorgeous. Nevertheless, Elizabeth believes she's ordinary looking. Within minutes of beginning our interview, she felt the need to tell me, "I'm really rather plain."

Elizabeth is also highly successful in her profession. She has garnered many prestigious awards for her professional work. She earns—with bonuses—over $300,000 a year. In addition, she spends hundreds of hours each year working, very quietly, for children's literacy. However, she is extremely modest regarding both her professional accomplishments and her community service contributions. She knows objectively what she has done with her life, but she seems to have difficulty identifying herself with her successes. It is as if she cannot admit that her own talent and hard work have brought her the successes she has achieved.

Elizabeth is an only child and is ambivalent about having children. She calls her mother in Boston, with whom she has always been close, once a week. She talks to her father every month or so. But this is not because he really wants to speak with her. Her father speaks with her when her mother puts him on the phone.

Today Elizabeth is pretty clear that her father's lack of validation has rubbed off on her in the form of her tendency to be unduly modest and even inappropriately self-effacing. In her interview with me, Elizabeth stressed that from the earliest memory right up to the present, her father has never praised her accomplishments. As an illustration, she described how she often brought home drawings from grade school. Her mother would attach the drawings with magnets to the refrigerator door. But, she said, "Invariably, my father took them down and threw them away. I used to think that if I tried harder and made a really good drawing, he'd allow it to stay. I know now nothing I did would ever have been good enough."

Her father is still withholding his affection and his approval. Recently Elizabeth was named Businesswoman of the Year by her state chamber of commerce. Her father didn't attend the banquet: he simply said that he was "too tired" to travel to the dinner. At first she was crushed by this continuing example of his inability to show approval, but ultimately she was able to put his disinterest in perspective and view it for what it was: a manifestation of his own inability to connect with her emotionally.

Now that Elizabeth has matured and received recognition from other sources, she has gained a better perspective on who she is and who her father is, and she has given up trying to please him. His decision to skip the chamber of commerce banquet was the final straw. According to Elizabeth, "That was it for me. He's always been too tired, and when it comes to showing any approval, he always will be. So I got to thinking it was time to put myself up for adoption, to get a new father. I've chosen a really nice widower who helps out at the literacy project. He listens and gives advice when I have problems on my job. He admires what I've done. He makes me laugh. I know I'm getting past the point where I might have children, but if I ever do, I'm going to ask him how he feels about being a grandfather."

This comment clearly indicates that Elizabeth has recognized that a child requires validation from her father. She has also recognized that she didn't get this validation from her own father, and that this was the result of his failure rather than her inadequacy. Finally, her response indicates that a part of her recovery from her father's failure to validate her existence was derived from validation she received through her subsequent, adult relationship with the widower at the literacy project.

"Just Being Myself Was Not Enough"

A common pattern of paternal failure is giving one's daughter approval not because she is intrinsically lovable but solely because she is a high achiever. The story of Karina illustrates the impact of such conditional approval, which she summed up with the observation that throughout her life, she always "thought that people valued me because of whatever I had last achieved, not because I was a warm and affectionate girl who was easy to be with."

Karina, a successful writer, is a beautiful, willowy woman in her early fifties who attracts admiring looks when she walks down the street. Karina told me that her father always set high standards for her and that she strived diligently to meet his expectations. She understands that the goals he set for her have made her driven to succeed in her career. She also believes that she has some understanding of the reasons that he acted as he did: "We all walk through the world with baggage, and my father's baggage was heavier than most."

Karina was born in Eastern Europe in a country under the tight control of communist rule. "We were a very close-knit family, really. Our little apartment was a sanctuary against the hostile world outside. It was the four of us against the world." But when Karina was six and her sister not much older, her father was imprisoned for two years for dissident activities. Her mother too was briefly put in jail.

"Years later," she told me, "one of his cellmates said that my father had worried about what his imprisonment was doing to the soul of his younger daughter. So he wasn't blind to the fact that I was a sensitive little girl in a way that my older sister was not. In pictures taken before they took him away, I'm rarely smiling. It was when they took my parents away that I started smiling. It was my armor, my way of softening people. After my parents were released and we were able to come to this country, I was the biggest smiler on the block. I didn't speak English, and that was my way to ingratiate myself. Even now, when I'm in tense situations, I smile a lot."

Her family arrived in the United States with nothing. Karina's mother and father both worked, the latter at a university in Washington, D.C., teaching the language he'd left behind.

"There wasn't much time left over for us children. They didn't want us to spend our lives as poor refugees. They wanted us to go to good schools. Because they were both so ferociously proud, they turned that whole prison thing into a positive force. 'Look at us, we prevailed, we survived with our heads held up.'

"Although my parents became totally assimilated, they were seen as very European by their circle of friends at the university and the State Department. At home we lived in a different world from my American world. It wasn't just that we spoke a different language. Our home was very European. Our things were old. My parents were very formal people, especially my father, cosmopolitan in their knowledge and taste. He could talk about pretty much anything: music, theater—and with great certainty. So there was never any doubt that this piece of music was the greatest piece of music. There was no room for negotiation there. Very antimodern. He was deeply rooted in the nineteenth century, early twentieth. But his cultivation was European, and that was my role model. I wanted to be elegant, cultivated, dignified.

"But one thing I didn't have from him was a sense of unconditional approval. I always thought—and this has stayed with me for my life—that people valued me because of whatever I had last achieved, not because I was a warm and affectionate girl who was easy to be with.

"I hugely admired him, but he was a role model as opposed to someone who offered closeness, coziness. He was not a physically affectionate person. I have no memory of sitting in his lap or holding his hand. I would have been very self-conscious doing that, because he was self-conscious about it. But I admired him and wanted to be like him. He was the bravest, most elegant, most dignified, cultivated man.

"His aloofness was a great motivator, a spur for me to try and get his approval. And I was never 100 percent sure that I had. He was embarrassed by others' emotions."

Karina's father was home for dinner every night. If he had a day off, it was a day spent with his family. Vacations too were family affairs, and when Karina's mother was unavailable, her father took either Karina or her sister to the diplomatic receptions to which he was so often invited.

"We thought we were very cool, watching Indian ladies in their saris and Africans in their robes. My father would show us off with great pride. I preened under that attention. He was also very proud of my academic achievements. I was always trying very hard to get those grades for him.

"Just being myself was not enough. I had to bring home the prizes to keep his affection. It was never unconditional. And I don't think you need to be a shrink to understand that that has kept me pushing for more achievements, because even now when someone is unexpectedly nice to me I think, 'Oh, they must have read my book,' or 'They saw the good reviews.' It can't just be because they like me. Even with my children, I feel I have to earn their love."

Karina's attempts to win her father's approval took her to the top of her profession as a writer, but it destroyed her first two marriages. Her father had always told her, "Be a success; don't marry one." But in the early, struggling days of her career, Karina had ignored him.

She describes her first husband as rich, intelligent, cultured, from an old Boston family—the epitome of the American dream for a young woman still not sure of her place in a new country. But like her father, Karina's husband "never could really open up. And I was way too immature. I was in my early twenties and desperate to make my mark in the world. I wanted to write books, get the success."

A writing assignment led to her second marriage. Sent to interview a man whose ego was as great as his fame, she fell in love and married him. "He replicated my father's withholding, but in a far more poisonous way. My father would never have gone silent for days if I just displeased him, as my second husband did—not only with me, but with our daughter. Very punishing, very punishing.

"I was madly in love with both my first and second husbands, but I see in retrospect that they were also a symbol of achievement . . . and of assimilation. They were proof that I'd arrived." Karina is still affected by the conditional approval that she received from her father. However, the success that she has enjoyed with her writing seems to have given her a somewhat more realistic perception of her intrinsic worth, and she has given considerable thought to the manner in which her insecurity influenced her behavior. She observed that it was her need for success that led her to choose each of her first two husbands, both of whom were very successful and neither of whom was supportive of her own striving. At this point in her life, however, Karina has been able to make a more mature choice.

Married for the third time, she laughs and says, "I guess to avoid confusion we should call Paul my 'current husband.'" She has come to rest in a more secure place: "Paul is a happy medium. He is a man of supreme achievement who is also very, very lovable and doesn't hide his feelings. He's the steadiest person I've ever known. You could set your clock by Paul. And yet if I'd met him when I was in my twenties, I never would have married him."

The need to achieve instilled in a daughter by a disapproving father who offers conditional acceptance is typically the strongest and most distinctive aspect of her personality. It is also one of the most resilient to change, in part because some of the fallout from this need is positive. Women who become successful because they feel that only their achievements matter often gain a sense of their intrinsic worth over time. These women often enter into problematic or even destructive relationships during early adulthood. With continued exposure to positive regard from others over the course of a lifetime, however, they tend to understand that they can please themselves as well as others. These women frequently form more appropriate, mutually rewarding relationships as they mature.

"Achieve, Achieve, Achieve"

It's hard to believe that Adrienna has just turned sixty. She is still the gamin, with huge brown eyes and short, shaggy hair. She has dressed for the interview in dark slacks and a loose red linen shirt, but as the afternoon lengthens and a chill enters the late autumn air, she pulls a throw from the back of the couch lined up against one wall of her studio and wraps it around her shoulders.

"Mediterranean blood," she explains, shivering. Even wrapped in this cashmere cocoon, Adrienna gives off sparks of energy as she admits that when she thinks of her late father, she feels nothing at all.

"When I try to think back, a lot of my childhood is a blank. I was probably a depressed child without knowing it. I'm not talking about when I was a teenager, because once I was out of the house, I had my friends. Once you have your friends, you're in a whole different world. You could drive around and hang out and talk on the phone for hours. But I don't have much recollection of life before that. I can describe the house where we lived. I can remember my father's sentimentality. I can even visualize him clearly. But he's still a shadowy figure. I don't have a concrete sense of him as a three-dimensional person."

Adrienna's father came to the United States from Italy when he was nine years old. He and his two younger sisters settled with their parents outside Boston.

"It was the basic immigrant story. Lots of hard work with my father selling vegetables off a cart, my grandfather putting the money they all earned into real estate and getting rich enough so he could send my father to Harvard, where he excelled, becoming a John Harvard Scholar, a sports champion in both handball and speed skating. My father got his law degree from Harvard, and when the Depression wiped out my grandfather's business, he took on responsibility for his two younger sisters, sending them to teacher's college."

It's like a Frank Capra movie: the poor Italian boy who climbs up in the world to become a star at Harvard, the bastion of WASPiness, his struggles rewarded by both business success and the hand of the princess.

"My mother's family back in Italy were minor royalty," Adrienna says. "When my parents fell in love, it was the union of the princess and the peasant. My mother was the youngest of eight kids. Her older sisters had married very rich guys, all of whom had gone to Harvard or Princeton. I think she married my father because she thought that with all his degrees, he'd become very rich too."

Although Adrienna's father was successful, she now describes him as incredibly insecure. "I think really my father hated his job and felt inadequate. I think he was a very insecure guy. All the achievements in the world didn't help him feel accepted in WASPy Connecticut, where we lived and where he felt he simply didn't belong. So he spent his life trying to further improve himself.

"My father liked to sit on the couch and read his law books from the minute he came home until the minute he went to bed. He would read his law books and listen to opera. So mainly I remember my father off by himself, reading. And then . . . nothing."

Although Adrienna feels that her father was always remote, she is also clear that he imposed his own incredible need to achieve on her. She explained that he made her feel that whatever she'd done wasn't good enough. In fact, she explained, "Both my parents constantly pushed me. Achieve, achieve, achieve.

"I never was able to please them, but I think some of that—at least with my father—was that he was never content with his own ability or performance. He once said to me, 'I wish I'd gone to Australia.' I think he never wanted to be a lawyer, but he had to survive. The Australia remark was him saying, 'I've never been happy.' It made a huge impression on me."

Adrienna did achieve. At school she was put into a program for intellectually gifted children and jumped up two grades. "The school recommended it," she says, "but it was terrible. I was much younger than the others, and my father wouldn't let me wear lipstick, though of course all the other girls did. Throughout this period, I remember that my parents were incredibly strict. I had to be home by ten when everybody else could be home by twelve—that kind of thing. As far as they were concerned, life wasn't about having fun; it was about achievement, and I was an extension of their ego."

Adrienna responded to the pressure by gathering together a group of friends. "I was terrified I wasn't going to get love unless I pleased people, so I tried to get everyone to like me. In large measure I succeeded; I was voted most popular in my class, best personality, and most likely to succeed.

"My parents had wanted me to go to Radcliffe, and my big rebellion was saying I wouldn't go there. So my father said, 'I'm not sending you to college unless you go to one of the Ivy League colleges.' I didn't want to pay for my own college, so I applied to Smith, Vassar, and Wellesley. I got into all of them, and I went to Smith. I should have gone to Radcliffe.

"I hated Smith. It was rural, and I was urban. It was freezing, and though Boston was only a little warmer, at least it was a city. I achieved well there, but I just loathed it. I had a battle with my father at Smith every semester. He would ask what courses I was taking and insisted I take music, which I almost failed because I hated it so. And he wanted me to take the big art history course, but I wouldn't do that because I was so viciously angry at him for telling me what to take."

After graduation Adrienna moved to New York City, where, despite her father's furious objections, she abandoned her background in literature and began to paint. To her astonishment, she was an instant success, with a gallery show her first year. "I never worked my way up," she says of the surprising speed that took her to the top of the art world.

In her second year in the city, she met and became engaged to a fellow artist. "I don't think I was really in love with him, but I just had to get married to get away from my parents. I thought they'd be very happy, but my father threw a fit."

Adrienna says it's ironic that after opposing the marriage, her parents fell in love with her husband—even more so after the birth of their son—although she points out that in the culture they both came from, males were more important than females. When the marriage eventually fell apart, it was her ex-husband who received more sympathy from their families.

"The thing that I did learn from my father was tremendous self-reliance. But the bad part of that is that I never allow myself to rely on anyone else. That's probably what broke up my marriage and the relationships that followed—until now.

"With Roger [Adrienna's second husband] it's totally different. When we became involved, he just said, 'Well, that's the way she's going to be. Why try to change the pattern at a later stage in life?' And he was right. I doubt if I could be different now. Roger is a very confident man who grew up with a mother who adored him. He said to me the other day, 'You've never been adored. I really adore you.' And I believe that. I am really happy talking to Roger about work, and he and I can have fun. I think the most fun I've had in my life is with Roger.

"Sometimes he says I don't take enough time to enjoy life. But—surprise—my enjoyment comes from achieving something for myself. When I'm painting and hit something right, I get so turned on that I do a little dance in my studio."

When I ask Adrienna if she thinks her father loved her, she sinks further down into the warmth of the blanket and gives a shake to her shaggy head, as though she's trying to knock loose a memory.

"As much as he was capable," she finally says, "and who knows how much that was? When I was successful in my career, he'd say, 'I'm so proud,' but it was more sentimentality speaking. Maybe I'm being unfair to him, and it was the real thing. I *cringe* when somebody gets sentimental. I was brought up to have a tough-girl attitude."

Adrienna often did precisely the opposite of what her father thought that she must do to become appropriately accomplished and to fit in. She became self-reliant, yet at the same time she clearly adopted her father's need to achieve. She still derives great pleasure from her professional successes. However, through the validation she received from the circle of friends she developed outside her family, she gradually learned to be able to allow herself to be loved for herself.

"Are You Going to Make Me a Birthday Cake?"

The story of Naomi illustrates still another way in which a disapproving father can invalidate his daughter. Naomi's father had a close relationship with her, particularly when she was very young. However, he was (and still is) an extremely rigid person who can view the world and his relationships in the world only through his own particularly narrow perspective regarding what is right and wrong, appropriate and inappropriate. Accordingly, the expectations that he has placed on Naomi have never taken into consideration her own feelings and thoughts. He has always told her exactly what to do to make him happy, exactly how to love him. And if she ever deviated from his demands, he has made her feel selfish for doing so. Naomi has never had a mutual give-and-take relationship with her father, and this has driven her crazy for her entire life.

"Until I was eleven or twelve I have more memories of my dad than of my mom," says Naomi. "He was the one who got up with me early in the morning, who taught me to write my name, so when I went to preschool I was able to sign myself in on the blackboard. He was a university professor, and when I was six, we went on sabbatical to Indonesia and lived in this teeny town where most people had never seen a foreigner—particularly not one like my dad who is six feet, three inches. We were like aliens."

In that foreign environment, Naomi's relationship with her father became even stronger. The two of them went off on frequent excursions, and later her father twice took Naomi with him on six-week trips to Asia. "We had a very strong relationship. I was really my dad's daughter."

The relationship changed dramatically Naomi was twelve and her parents divorced. Naomi explained that when she learned of the impending divorce, "I was beside myself. I threw myself on the floor in a temper tantrum. My mom is a counselor, and she's trained to make a lot of space for irrational emotions and anger. My dad is a scientist, logical and rational. He'd try to reason with me, and the situation would become very explosive. He wasn't good at anticipating what would set me off. I think my father really didn't want to get a divorce and that it was my mother who precipitated it. It must have been a double blow to him—first he loses his wife and then his daughter, who used to think he was great and who spent a lot of time with him.

"My relationship with my father was never the same after that. It must have been very hard for him, and the problems in our relationship have continued into adulthood. A lot of that is no longer about the divorce but who he is as a person.

"My father has to call the shots. It's not so much a relationship as a command performance: 'Call me every Sunday.' 'Are you going to make me a birthday cake?' He has to tell you what he wants you to do, and if I don't do it, it's because I'm really selfish. He doesn't yell. It's all very measured and logical. It makes me crazy, and I become a child again, hysterical. I get really, really upset. I can't show him I love him my way. It has to be his, or he'll be 'disappointed.'"

Naomi understands why her father is as rigid as he is. She attributes her father's need for control to the fact that his father is bipolar. "He had a horrible go of it," she says. "I think living with someone who's bipolar creates a sense of chaos; you can't control anything, so you want to control everything. And not enough love. I don't think he felt much love from his father, and when my grandfather would show it, it would be in a material way, buying stuff, and that was scary because it was part of his being on the way up into a manic phase."

Although Naomi is able to understand, and to a certain extent rationalize, what causes her father's controlling behavior, as you listen to her talk, you can hear the hurt child lingering inside, still angry at the father she had idolized. She acknowledges that her father loves her but says, "I don't feel loved the way I think I should be."

Today Naomi is happily married, the mother of a small child, and successful in her career. But to this day, she finds herself bending over backward to comply with whatever demands her father might make on her, and she still feels frustrated because he will not allow her to love him in the way that feels right to her.

"Chasing After a Man Who Is Looking Away from Me"

Deborah's father was narcissistic and completely self-absorbed as she was growing up. He wanted and expected to be taken care of, and he had little use for any of his six children. Deborah said that her mother was at least interested in the children, but that her father was interested only in the news and the stock market.

Today Deborah understands that her father's lack of interest or approval has affected her orientation toward men in a significant manner. She married and then divorced a man who was sensitive but unsuccessful, and to this day, she finds it difficult to allow the possibility that a man can be both emotionally connected and competent.

Deborah explained, "My father was very remote. He was a Wall Street stockbroker, but he was very withholding when it came to money." Deborah told me that she could remember "making efforts to engage him, trying to make of him a daddy, like my idealized image of an American dad—like the TV show *Gidget*, where the main parent was the father and there was no mother, and the show always began with Gidget talking about how a problem had been resolved when she talked to her father. I would watch *Gidget* avidly, but my father was never like hers. He roared; he had obsessions. If he couldn't find one of his pencils, the whole house went into a mode of emergency, and we had to look for it."

Deborah described her family as "a tightly run German Jewish family, Orthodox but with a German emphasis on order and quiet. "My father was what today you'd call a news junkie—cerebral, somewhat overweight, sitting hours upon hours with the *Wall Street Journal*, the *Financial Times*, the *New York Times*. English was his third language, and both my parents were very language conscious. He loved words and kept lists of those he'd come across in his reading in his sort of obsessive handwriting."

Deborah is a writer who had early success writing fiction but has now shifted to more analytical essays, a change she thinks was an attempt to move toward her father's world. "I love critical writing, but I probably also thought that was the most acceptable to him, a smart mind commenting on issues. Or maybe I just didn't have enough ego to continue writing fiction," says the woman who admits, "I think I saw my father as proof that men wouldn't find me attractive. I used him as a kind of litmus test. Could I intrigue a man? No. I felt I was of no interest."

With a father who either ignored her or diminished her, Deborah grew up feeling uncomfortable with emotionally open men. "My template of what it was to be male was to be closed off emotionally, not know how to boil water, and to be catered to. My father had very little ability to show love, and I don't know if he did love. He was mind-bogglingly self-absorbed—a big, pampered child—and my mother encouraged this."

In an attempt to break with her upbringing, Deborah married her father's opposite: a man who "had developed a side of himself that was the feminine; he could cook, he could do everything my brothers and fathers could not do, like change a light bulb. I think I also found him artistic. I probably didn't count on how much it would bother me—not the lack of money but the lack of direction."

Or the disdain her father openly showed to her own husband. They divorced, and today Deborah says, "There is a whole side of me that verges on anti-male. I'm certainly a feminist, but I also think I took in that what matters is whether my father would notice. I sometimes feel it's an effort that will never be gratified, that I'll always be chasing after this man who's looking away from me."

Deborah, with her analytical mind, noted that a father like hers who ignores his daughter sometimes produces a woman unable to flirt: "My sister and I are the least flirty people you could meet, but I find it fascinating that friends of mine who are no more attractive assume people will be interested in them. I think that to flirt, you need to have the confidence established in your own mind that you're intrinsically of interest to the person."

Flirting is to give consequence to the inconsequential, to have one conversation on the surface while a provocative and unspoken one slides along beneath. A daughter whose father never even listened to the words on the surface will find it hard to believe a man might hear those that aren't spoken.

Thus, Deborah has a degree of understanding regarding the manner in which her uninvolved and disapproving father has affected her life with respect to both her career and her relationships. However, she doesn't seem to have gone as far as some of the other women discussed in this chapter in terms of establishing a strong sense of self and developing mutually satisfying adult relationships.

"Why Can't He Accept My Sexuality?"

Maura is a twenty-eight-year-old who works as a stagehand in Broadway and off-Broadway theaters in New York. She has always wanted to work in the theater, and she majored in theater arts at a prestigious woman's college in New England. After graduation, she moved to New York, and she showed remarkable strength of character and determination in securing entry into the stagehands union, which is difficult for anyone to get into—and nearly impossible for a woman. Through hard work and dedication, she has gained the acceptance of her fellow workers and is very happy in her work.

Maura is a lesbian who became aware of her sexual orientation at the age of fourteen, after a period of struggling to understand why she did not feel attracted to boys as did most of her girlfriends. She had always been a joy for her parents, never getting into trouble and doing well in school. She had felt loved by both her parents, whom she perceived as taking great pride in her looks, her personality, and her diligence. When Maura became quite certain of her sexual orientation, she simply informed them both. She had no idea that this disclosure would have any impact on how they felt about her.

But it did. She could see immediately that both of them were disappointed. Her mother accepted what Maura was saying, but she also expressed disappointment because she would not have the grandchildren she was looking forward to having.

Maura's dad could not accept the disclosure. At first he dismissed it as a childish phase, suggesting, "All young girls go through a period during which they think they are attracted to women, but they grow out of it." As time went by, however, he began to realize that Maura might in fact be a lesbian. And when this reality began to sink in, his whole attitude toward her changed.

First, her father asked Maura not to be "too obvious" about her "choice." He said that he would be embarrassed to have everyone in town know that she was gay, even if she did eventually get over it. He told her that she could not bring her "girlfriends" to their house, and he urged her not to go out on dates in places where people who knew him would see her "holding hands with another girl."

Over time, his negative response to Maura's sexual orientation began to generalize to other aspects of her life. Soon he was attributing her lesbianism to her interest in the theater, and he no longer wanted to go to see the high school productions that she acted in, directed, or staged. He criticized her decision to major in theater arts in college, and he made sarcastic remarks about the college she chose, suggesting that it was the "intellectual capital of the Daughters of Sappho." He asked her at one point why she couldn't choose a regular profession for a modern woman, such as a district attorney or a stockbroker. He generally regarded these kind of comments as "good-natured humor." However, when Maura told him how much they hurt her, he became angry, claiming that she had a "very thin skin" and suggesting that she wouldn't react so strongly if she didn't feel deep down that she was making a mistake.

Even worse, Maura's dad became increasingly less affectionate toward her. The big bear hugs that she had loved became a thing of the past. She even thought that he showed signs of contempt when he looked at her.

Her father's inability to accept her sexual orientation threw her for loop. She found herself from time to time wishing that she were not a lesbian, something that had never occurred to her while she was in the process of trying to sort out her sexual feelings. She became depressed and felt that she was undergoing a process of grieving for a lost father. "It was almost as if he had died," she said.

She had a period of nearly a year during which she withdrew from many of her activities, and her grades suffered. It was only the understanding of some of her high school teachers that kept her emotional crisis from jeopardizing her chances of attending her first choice among the colleges to which she applied.

Fortunately, Maura received a great deal of support and understanding from her friends at school, both straight and gay. They attributed her father's response to his age and to the fact that "you can't teach an old dog new tricks." They told her that she should try to understand where he was coming from, but at the same time she shouldn't let his old prejudices "mess up her head." Although it was difficult at first for her to try to follow this advice, their continued support and encouragement helped her to work it through.

Eventually Maura got back on an even keel and pursued her interests with the same diligence and enthusiasm that she had shown for her entire life. She felt completely accepted for who she was at college and among her colleagues in the theater in New York. She is doing well professionally and socially. She has not yet found her ideal life partner, but she has had several meaningful relationships, and she continues to date and share her life with people she feels she can trust and rely on—people to whom she can feel close.

Maura still has a very close relationship with her mother, and her relationship with her father is improving. He is becoming more accepting over time, partially due to being exposed to more lesbian women, whom Maura is now allowed to bring home with her on vacations and holidays. Maura says that she will always feel somewhat betrayed by her dad because of his initial response to her disclosure, but she also acknowledges that with the help of her friends, she has learned to accept him for what he is. She gives him credit for "making the progress that he has."

The Path to Recovery

The women described in this chapter share the relentless failure of their fathers to provide unconditional love and approval. They share as well the natural response to their fathers, which is to try harder and harder to please him by achieving more and more. Ironically the fathers who fail so miserably at the task of helping their daughters develop healthy positive self-concepts succeed very well at producing daughters who are high achievers.

The daughters are controlled by the need to please. They keep trying to be perfect. They are good students. They are often well liked. But they don't feel good about themselves. They refuse to admit that they are attractive, or intelligent, or successful, or lovable. They often get involved with men who cannot feel or display emotion, because this is the kind of man with whom they grew up.

Fortunately, most of these women come to recognize the reality that as great as their successes may be, they will never satisfy their dad. This realization may come relatively early or not until quite late in life, but when it comes, it is truly liberating. Moreover, many of these women with disapproving fathers begin to obtain the validation they need from other sources. In some cases, a loving mother will compensate for the failure of the disapproving father. In that case, the dynamic of achieving success without giving oneself credit may never play out. But in other cases, this validation comes from peers during adolescence, from teachers during adolescence and young adulthood, or from colleagues in the employment setting. As these women come to feel validated, they begin to realize that they are lovable. At this point, they often find supportive, loving partners.

The clear lesson to be learned from the stories of the women in this chapter is that if you are a woman who feels unworthy of being loved and never gives herself credit for her personal accomplishments, you need to pay very careful attention to what the people around you are telling you about yourself.

Just because your father never told you that you were beautiful, warm, loving, intelligent, or hard working does not mean that all of these things are not true. And when you receive affection and praise from those around you, do not dismiss it out of hand. Once you begin to believe the positive things that others are saying about you, you will feel better about yourself and allow yourself to participate in relationships of all kinds that are mutually rewarding. At that point, you will be well along the road to allowing yourself to be loved.

Chapter Two

The Mentally Ill Father

Daughters who have a mentally ill father are at increased risk of developing psychosocial difficulties of their own. This is to some degree the result of genetic factors. Some forms of mental illness do run in families. However, the adverse impact of a father's mental illness on his daughter is more heavily dependent on aspects of the father's behavior and prevailing social attitudes regarding mental illness.

Depending on the diagnosis, a father who is mentally ill may behave erratically. His daughter won't know what to expect or when trouble might arise. This unpredictability tends to produce anxiety, particularly social anxiety regarding the dependability of relationships. This anxiety is particularly likely to occur in those families in which the father's mental illness produces long periods of absence during necessary hospitalizations.

When fathers have bipolar illness, for example, unpredictable absences are common during the manic phases of their illness. Daughters who grow up knowing that their fathers cannot be depended on often generalize this experience to all men. As a result, they may unconsciously avoid developing serious attachments to men. Or they may develop attachments but live in constant worry that their attachment figures will abandon them without warning.

The homes of mentally ill fathers also tend to be chaotic when they are there. Often there is tension or even hostility between father and mother, since women with mentally ill husbands are often forced to take on all responsibility for financing and running the household. The one-sided delegation of responsibility may leave mothers with too little time to devote to parenting. It may also leave them physically exhausted and emotionally depleted, too tired to keep the household running smoothly and dependably and too numb to nurture close relationships with the children.

In many instances, daughters in the homes of mentally ill fathers wind up assuming much of the responsibility for running the home because there is no one else to do the task. Older daughters may also assume much of the responsibility for meeting the needs of their younger siblings. This situation tends to produce adult women who are nurturing toward others but have great difficulty allowing themselves to relax and enjoy life.

When a daughter is just a little girl at the onset of the father's mental illness, she may not understand why he is acting the way that he does and assume that she is somehow at fault. This is particularly true because mental illness carries a stigma. Her mother may deny her husband's condition altogether or fail to explain his unpredictable behavior. As the daughter gets older, the social stigma associated with mental illness may also lead her to avoid having friends over to her home, for fear that her dad will do something odd or that it will otherwise become evident that everything is not right in the home. Such a daughter may become socially isolated. She may also tend to shy away from involvement in school and community activities where fathers tend to be present or participate.

I interviewed four women who made it quite clear that their fathers had a significant psychiatric diagnosis. One woman was the daughter of a father with schizophrenia, another grew up with a father who had obsessive-compulsive personality disorder, and the other two had fathers with manic-depressive disorders.

One of these women, Rachel, also had a narcissistic mother, leaving her pretty much without any source of emotional support, approval, or validation. The second woman, Gail, did feel loved by her father, despite his erratic behavior and outbursts of anger. Perhaps as a result of feeling loved or perhaps as a result of maternal support, Gail appears better adjusted as an adult.

The specific problems these four women experienced during childhood and adolescence were quite different, as were the symptoms of their fathers' diagnoses. However, elements of their individual responses to their fathers' behavior were similar, and each experienced some difficulty in social relationships during adolescence and early adulthood.

Common elements appear as well in the daughters' long-term adjustment and recovery from the effects of their father's mental illness. Each of these women had to come to understand that her father was ill, that she was in no way to blame for the illness, and that most people in the world would understand the difficulties she had experienced if she could simply muster the strength to disclose them.

"My Dad Was F___ing Nuts"

I had spoken with Cora on the telephone a few days before our interview, and she had asked for some idea about what I was studying and how I planned to use the stories I gathered. I must have mentioned the term "unavailable father" to her when we spoke on the telephone, because when we sat down to talk, her first words were, "My father was unavailable all right. My dad was unavailable because my dad was f___ing nuts."

From that point, Cora spoke without a word from me for several minutes, giving me some examples of just how crazy her dad was. She continued, "I don't mean a little odd or neurotic. I mean full-blown f___ing off the wall bizarre, with voices talking to him, visions of God appearing, and fantasies that the local police had wire-tapped the house. When he was out of the hospital and around the house, which was mercifully rare, you just never knew what he might do.

"One time when I was about fifteen, Dad came out of the house into the midst of a backyard barbecue wearing nothing but a trench coat and a wool hat with earflaps at half-staff. Before we could round him up and get him back inside, he had gone around to some relatives, whom he had known for his entire life, asking them whether they were spying for the government and whether we should have to feed them when they were already getting paid by the military intelligence people to keep track of his whereabouts.

"He really freaked everyone out, because each time he would ask someone a question, he would first receive the question he was to ask from some unseen and unheard source that appeared to exist somewhere in the sky. Dad would have a one-sided conversation with this unknown source regarding exactly how each question should be phrased and to whom it should be addressed. Some of the adults found the whole incident funny (in an uncomfortable sort of way). But sometimes there were small children there as well, and they just didn't know what to make of it."

Cora's father had appeared to be relatively normal throughout high school. He was a decent athlete and an average student. He had no aspirations to go to college and had instead enlisted in the army, hoping to become an Airborne Ranger. Right after he finished basic training, he had married Cora's mom, his high school sweetheart. She became pregnant with Cora immediately. When Cora was born in 1966, her dad was in Vietnam.

Cora's dad had a breakdown while he was overseas. He was shipped back to the states and placed in a military hospital, where he was diagnosed as having schizophrenia. He spent about three months in the hospital that first time. The doctors said that with the medication they were giving him, he was "stabilized" and could go home. He returned to the small town where they lived, and some relatives pulled a few strings to get him a job working on the country road crew, filling potholes, plowing snow, and clearing debris from the roads.

Cora explained, "Dad worked for the road crew throughout my childhood, but his schizophrenia never really went away, and from time to time he had to be hospitalized. He nearly lost his job a few times, but what with being a veteran and having a diagnosis, they made allowances and kept him on for twenty years until he retired in 1988. That was when I was twenty-two.

"The problems that Dad had over the years all came from his not taking his medication when he was supposed to. Each time he would go into the hospital, they would get him more or less straightened out with the medication, and he would keep taking it for a while after he came home. Then he would be able to go to work and do what he was supposed to do. But he was never happy on the medication. He said that it took away his feelings and made him feel like a Zombie. So he keep taking the medicine for a while—I mean sometimes as long as a year or more—but in the end, he would always stop taking it, and then pretty soon he'd be hearing voices again and behaving like the nut that he was.

"It was really sad for me, because when he was on the medicine, he was kind of shut down, with no emotion. He didn't seem to care very much about what I was doing or what my younger brother was doing. When he did show some feelings, it was kind of painful for everyone, because we could see that he really did love us, but we also knew that he was off his meds and soon there would be an incident.

"His schizophrenia made life difficult at home. Mom worked at a convenience store in town and occasionally as a teacher's aide in the elementary school, but she had a difficult time working steadily because so often she would have to drop everything to take care of Dad when he had one of his crazy periods. In some ways it was better when he was at the hospital, because at least then I knew what to expect at home. But I got saddled with a lot of extra work helping out with the housework and taking care of my younger brother. Even so, I don't know what we could have done if it had not been for the fact that we lived in a small town with both my mom's family and my dad's family. There were times when everybody pitched in to help, especially during crises.

"I felt obligated to help cope with the situation as much as I could, and as a result, I probably gave up on some things in school. I never went out for cheerleading or school plays, and I was a kind of halfhearted student. Needless to say, I didn't throw any parties at my house. But I did have some friends who understood, and I have those same friends to this day. I didn't have any trouble finishing school, but I didn't excel either. So after I finished school I lived at home and got a job at the office of the local vet. I got married within a year after high school to a local builder, and we began to raise a family. It was a good thing I married a builder too, because before too long, he was working on the large two-family home where we now live. Of course (if you haven't already guessed), Mom and Dad live in the other apartment.

"Dad is still on and off his medication, and it is pretty clear to everyone that he is 'not quite right' most of the time. But as he's gotten older, he has tended to be on his medicine more than off it, and we haven't had to put him back in the hospital for some time now. My kids, who are grown up now, had a few problems understanding their grandfather's craziness, but I was very careful to explain the whole situation to them early on, and they too benefited from the acceptance they received from family and friends in our small town.

"All things considered, I can't really complain. I do wonder what might have been if I had felt a little more freedom to get involved and take some risks when I was in school. Who knows, I might have gone to college, become an astronaut, or married an ambassador. But probably not. And I do have a really nice home."

What we see here with Cora is close to a best-case scenario for the daughter of a father with schizophrenia. Cora had some embarrassing moments during her childhood, but her father was never violent or abusive (as some schizophrenics can be), and he was never a serious substance abuser (as many schizophrenics become).

Cora assumed some responsibilities during adolescence that are well beyond the norm. Her social life was clearly restricted, and she may indeed have forgone opportunities that might have expanded her horizons and led her down more adventurous paths. But she was fortunate to have a mother who was both unimpaired and responsible, and the family benefited greatly from the emotional and tangible support that they received from their families and friends. She also seems to have found a good man who has helped her build a solid family of her own.

"I Was Constantly Walking on Eggshells"

Chely is a twenty-seven-year-old fifth-grade teacher who has been married to a landscape contractor for two years. They are just beginning to think about having children. Chely feels that she has come a long way to get to this point in her life, because throughout high school, she was not at all sociable and often wondered if she would ever have a career, get married, and have children. Looking back, she realizes that it was primarily her father's psychiatric disorder that made it very difficult for her to have a normal teenage social life.

Chely's father was never diagnosed professionally, but based on her reading, it's quite clear to Chely now that her father had an obsessive-compulsive personality disorder. Having heard her story, I agree completely with her informal diagnosis.

Chely told me that for as long as she could remember, her father, the sole proprietor of a small jewelry store, was a perfectionist. He was always impeccably dressed. He always opened and closed his business at precisely the times listed on the door. He expected dinner to be served at 6:30 each evening, and he expected everyone to be at the table on time and in clean clothes. Chely said that her father demanded that everything in the house be not just clean and neat, but also organized in exactly the manner that he thought it should be. She told me, "If there was a pillow on the couch that wasn't lined up right where he thought it should be, then someone was going to have to explain to him why it had been moved in the first place and why it had not been returned 'correctly' to its proper place."

Chely told me that her father was so intent on having everything in its proper place that he often spent hours looking around the house for things that weren't as they should be. This checking activity took up a great deal of his time, to the point that he often did not have time to engage his family socially. Vacations were only possibilities that were discussed; they never actually took place. In her entire childhood, Chely had never gone on a family picnic or a trip to the beach. These were events in which she participated only when friends invited her to join with their families.

Her father's primary leisure activity was playing by himself with his model railroad layout, which took up the entire basement of their home. He spent hours oiling the trains and cleaned the setup each day with a tiny vacuum cleaner. He also spent hours keeping a journal in which he recorded the serial number of each piece of model railroad equipment that he acquired, along with the date it was manufactured, the date he purchased it, the cost, and each date that he oiled it or otherwise maintained the item. He attended model railroad shows and was an officer in the National Association of Model Railroaders.

It was very difficult for anyone to tear him away from this little world of model trains. Chely recalled an occasion when she was eleven when her father had agreed with her mother that they would go to a school play in which Chely was performing. When it came time to leave for the school, however, Chely's father discovered that he had misplaced a piece of documentation for one of his model engines. Unable to leave the house until he found the paper, he searched for more than an hour until he found it: Chely's mother had to take her to the play herself, and her father never showed up at all.

On another occasion, Chely's younger brother accidentally dropped one of the locomotives. The train wasn't seriously damaged, but it did get "a little scratch near the cow-catcher." Chely's father first tried to remove the scratch by carefully buffing the engine some fine steel wool, but he discovered that he could not actually make the blemish disappear. Although no one else would ever have noticed the tiny flaw, Chely's father sold the engine to a fellow hobbyist at a loss and then proceeded to buy a new one to replace it. He also made it very clear to her brother, "the perpetrator of the damage," that this was not an incident that could be easily forgotten or forgiven.

Chely's father was not harsh in punishing his children for their misdeeds, but he was extremely meticulous in pointing them out. He was moralistic and believed in obeying the letter of the law. He never exceeded the speed limit, even when Chely's mom was in labor with her brother. If her father parked at a meter and found he didn't have the necessary change, he wouldn't leave the car there even long enough to make change at the shop next door.

He set strict curfews for his children and more often than not refused to give them permission to go on school trips because he knew that "kids often get into mischief on those trips." On one occasion a major family battle erupted when Chely's father refused to allow her younger brother to go away for the weekend on a scout camping trip, because that would mean missing that week's Sunday school and church.

Chely's father assigned weekly chores to each of the children. These chores were not unreasonable, but the children had nothing to say about what the chores might be. Her father simply decided what needed to be done and informed them of his decisions at dinner. Chely had to clean up after supper and wash the dishes. Her brother had to cut the grass, weed the garden, and rake leaves. But her father made these tasks into an issue because, as she put it, "After you were done, he would come around and check to see that you had done it 'right.' And I'm not talking about making sure that the dishes were really clean. I could have understood that. But he made sure that I put each plate back exactly where it had come from. He made sure that the plates were stacked neatly in the cupboard. He even checked to see that unused paper napkins had been neatly returned to the cellophane wrapper in which they came from the store." Chely said that she got to be so afraid that she would do something wrong that she was afraid to do anything at all.

Chely told me that her father's obsessive behavior, his rigid rules, and his constant checking up had the effect of making her "afraid of my own shadow." It wasn't that she feared that he would hit her or even punish her severely. But she always knew that if she deviated even slightly from the prescribed behaviors, he would make a great show of his disappointment and suggest that she was indeed an inconsiderate child for behaving in a manner that was clearly destined to upset him. Chely explained how he made her feel: "It was like, the only way to do things correctly is my way, and if you fail to do things as I want them done, you have stabbed me in the heart. I felt like I was constantly walking on eggshells, waiting for something to break. If I had ever broken a dish, it would have been like breaking his heart or delivering some kind of mortal wound. And the same thing applied to overstaying a curfew or participating in some activity that he disapproved.

"Needless to say, during my high school years, I was never the life of the party. In fact, my father made it very difficult or even impossible for me to have what most teens would consider a normal social life. My girlfriends didn't come around to my house, because I was clearly anxious that they might break something or make a mess. Understandably this made them uncomfortable. Often I couldn't participate in activities at their houses either because my father considered the activities (such as slumber parties) as likely to lead to trouble or because he would want me home long before any of the other girls.

"I hardly ever dated for essentially the same reasons. I certainly couldn't imagine a boyfriend having to meet my dad and attempt to have a normal conversation with him. I was sure that any boy who talked to my father would consider him weird and determine that dating me was just not worth the discomfort associated with seeing my father.

"So it really wasn't until I went away to college that I began to loosen up. Once I was out of the house, I could begin to put the situation at home in perspective. It was one of my roommates who first suggested that my father had an obsessive-compulsive personality disorder. I always knew that he was different from other fathers in ways that were difficult to deal with, but I was really excited to learn that his different behavior was actually a psychiatric disorder with a name. I couldn't wait to take psychology to learn more about his disorder and my response to it. Gradually I realized that I didn't have to spend the rest of my life walking on eggshells. I began to socialize. I went on dates. And ever so slowly I moved in the direction of normality.

"I went on to become an elementary school teacher, and to this day I take a certain amount of pleasure in the fact that my job occasionally requires me to get my hands dirty. I actually enjoy the chaotic atmosphere in the classroom. I also married a man who is anything but neat. In fact, John is a slob. His job has him up to his elbows in dirt all day, and he plays football with his friends on weekends. He gets muddy, and he wears dirty sweatshirts. We entertain, and sometimes we don't clean up until the next day. We go on vacation. We are going to have kids, and we are going to let them do the things that they really want to do, even if they get dirty and break things."

So here we have another example of a woman whose father's psychiatric condition made her childhood and adolescence difficult and interfered with her normal social development. In this case, Chely began to realize how screwed-up things had been at home only after she got some distance from the problem and a reality check from some new friends who could listen to her story objectively and direct her toward information that helped her to understand where she had come from and why she had some of the difficulties that she experienced.

"He Had Such Highs and Lows"

Gail is forty-four years old and is married, with two children. She is a partner in a small restaurant, and her husband is a chiropractor. She considers herself well adjusted, happily married, and successful. However, Gail acknowledges that she had a difficult childhood due to her father's mental illness. Gail's description of her father leaves little doubt that he suffered from bipolar disorder. She explained, "We never talked about it, and I'm not sure that he ever acknowledged a definitive diagnosis of bipolar disorder. But it was obvious. He had such extremes—times when he was on top of the world, so euphoric, and then the times when he was really down." Several times in his life, he has been so depressed that he required psychiatric treatment.

Her father's mood swings have made his life an unpredictable roller-coaster ride. Over the course of his lifetime, he went through four wives and at least a dozen different employers. He also formed and then discarded a series of friendships. During his manic episodes, he fell in love, became wildly enthusiastic about new business opportunities, and quickly formed close relationships with new friends who shared in his temporary interests and endeavors. During his depressive periods, the wives with whom he had fallen in love suddenly became "not good enough" for him. The new jobs and business ventures that seemed so exciting and promising turned up hollow and left him angry and disappointed. And the new friends proved to be shallow and disloyal.

Gail was the product of her father's first marriage, the first of two children. She describes her father as loving toward her mother and loving as well toward her and her brother for "most of the eleven years that we were together as a family." During this period, her father was a regional head of marketing for a large electronics firm. She remembers seeing lots of pictures of him taken with celebrities who endorsed the products he sold, and she even has some vague memories of him talking very enthusiastically to friends about stereos and televisions and new home entertainment systems.

During this period, he was making good money, and the family was comfortable. However, even then he had some pretty serious mood swings. He would be fine for weeks or months, and then for a week or so he would get depressed, moody, and uncommunicative. The depressive episodes were stressful for everyone in the family. Gail described them as being "like one day he was there, and the next day he was gone—off in his own little world."

When Gail was ten, her father fell apart completely. It seemed to Gail that one day he was happy in work, and the next day he was miserable. Overnight the products he marketed became inferior and his colleagues at work became inept backstabbers. He started missing work. At first he called in sick a lot, but then he simply stopped going. He just stayed at home. Gail's mother tried to be supportive, but she fell out of favor as well. Gail distinctly remembers an argument between her father and mother in which her father told his mother that his job was meaningless, his life was meaningless, and their relationship was "just not good enough for me." Gail noted that this argument was particularly distressing because her father spoke these words without anger, almost without any affect at all. Shortly after, he was hospitalized with severe depression.

When he was released the hospital a few months later, his mood was much better. He was taking antidepressants, which clearly helped. But the doctors hadn't yet figured out that he was bipolar.

Within a few weeks of getting out of the hospital, Gail's father had launched himself into a new business venture, which involved some medical applications of electronic technology. He was away from home most of the time. He had a partner who became his new best friend, and he pretty much ignored his wife and children. Soon he became involved with another woman, to whom Gail refers as "the one he left us for."

Although Gail felt abandoned when her father left, her mother was neither surprised nor devastated. In fact, she had prepared for this eventuality both financially and emotionally. She had returned to work when she realized that her husband's mood swings could jeopardize his employment. She had also developed a support network of friends with whom she shared the difficulties of living with a man with such mood swings.

The cyclical pattern of mania and depression was repeated throughout her father's life, resulting in four marriages, multiple short-lived business ventures, and a bevy of confused and disgruntled former "best friends." Gail indicated that her father sought help for his psychiatric condition on a number of occasions and was hospitalized several times, but he never really accepted the idea that he was bipolar and never consistently took any of the medications that were prescribed for him over the years. He died several years ago of an unrelated heart ailment. In retrospect, Gail feels both sympathy for her father's difficult life and sadness regarding the loss of the much better relationship that they might have had.

"He had a chemical imbalance, and he needed something to stabilize the terrible mood swings. Even though the public acceptance of mental illness has come a long way, still to this day you can't talk about it. You have to sweep it into the closet. If my father had a chronic physical ailment instead of a mental problem, maybe he could have stayed on whatever medicine he needed.

"He was ashamed of it, and it's so sad. Life would have been better if he had been able to accept that his mental illness was a genetic disability. It wasn't anything that he did. It was tumultuous. It was up and down. I remember writing him letters long after my parents divorced, pouring out my feelings, urging him to take his medications. But he couldn't accept anything that he didn't want to hear."

Gail believes that despite his difficulties, her father did love her. They maintained contact after her parents were divorced and throughout the course of his life. Although his continuing illness tended to make their communication irregular and unpredictable, Gail understood the problem and accepted that the relationship would simply be on and off according to the phase of her father's illness. In spite of his travails, Gail feels that her father did manage to communicate his love for her.

"And now he is gone, and I miss him . . . and I feel bad because now I know there will never be any chance to make things right."

Gail has been resilient in the face of her father's manic-depressive episodes. In part, this is because she experienced enough of his loving side to know that he cared for her and valued her as a person. In addition, Gail's mother's resilience in the face of her husband's illness provided Gail with consistency and security despite her father's ups and downs. In addition, Gail came to understand that her father had bipolar disorder and that his mood swings were never adequately stabilized medically. Therefore, she could accept that he simply did what he could to show his love when he could.

Gail's understanding of her father's medical condition as the underlying cause of his unpredictability also seems to have enabled her to develop an image of the ideal male distinct from her conception of her father. Gail chose and remains happily married to a man whom she describes as quite different from her father: consistently positive, affectionate, and reliable.

"Trying to Be the One Thing
My Parents Could Feel Good About"

Rachel is an attractive forty-five-year-old who is a partner in a public relations firm, where her people-pleasing skills have brought her considerable success. She has the perfect figure of a woman who was a competitive swimmer in college and still swims two or three times a week. Rachel's father, like Gail's, suffered from bipolar disorder. But Rachel's experience was quite different from Gail's.

Rachel's father was the head of the international division of a large investment bank. A bright and well-educated man, he had held important government posts at a young age and for a number of years was a powerful figure in the hierarchy of the bank. However, when the bipolar disorder set in, he became alternately angry and depressed. He had periods of nonproductivity and experienced difficulty getting along with his colleagues at the bank.

Rachel explained that because of his mood swings, "My father was basically thrown out of his firm. There was a boardroom battle, and I think my father was probably maniacally arrogant. He was shoved upstairs to be vice chairman, and that was really the writing on the wall. I remember we went to Scotland on a vacation, and he threw out his medicine and said, 'Life is going to be better.' And that did *not* happen. As I recollect, he spent the next year in his office at home in his pajamas.

"That's when I remember seeing the mania. At that time we had a house in Southampton [New York], and during one of his manic phases, he built an entire room in the basement almost overnight. He just built a room," Rachel sighs, remembering the intensity of his project, "all night—all weekend."

Eventually Rachel's father was diagnosed with bipolar disorder, and the physicians put him on lithium. This had the desired effect of reducing the mood swings, but it had devastating side effects. On the medication, he was there physically, but emotionally and mentally he was a man who had shut down.

Rachel told me about a dream she had as a child in which her father appeared. Rachel saw him as though he was floating up out of a dream and she called him the "wooden man": "There were curtains in my bedroom, and I remember thinking, in that half-awake dream state, that my father was a wooden man who had come out of the curtains—like, you know, the art school mannequins that are made out of wood. He looked like that, or like a wooden shoehorn, scooping me up when he'd come to get me out of bed. I guess I thought of him as just barely living, a presence without emotion."

Several years after her father was diagnosed, her parents' marriage fell apart. She told me, "When my parents got divorced, my father was off sleeping with other women, and of course my mother made it worse, because she was saying, 'Look how horrible your father is.' She didn't try to explain it to me.

"My father's condition and his affairs were very hard on my mother, but she's also narcissistic and was flagrantly having affairs of her own. At the time of the divorce, she was sleeping with an old family friend. It was a long-standing affair. All the kids on both sides, we all knew about it as we grew up. So the divorce was really hard on my father too." Rachel's older sister was away at school when the divorce occurred, so "I got the parents and she escaped."

Rachel suggested that as a result of the disintegration of her family, she became a "complete people pleaser. To this day, I worry about it if I don't get an e-mail back from somebody. Are they mad at me? I mean, it's just the most typical knee-jerk reactions, like, Did I do something wrong?

"Obviously as a young girl when your father's not available, you think it's your fault. You want to please. I became a complete overachiever, trying to be the one thing that my parents could feel good about. I remember being in college driving in my car, sobbing, because I felt that I had to be the most perfect thing in the world, so my parents could say, 'My life is blown to hell, my marriage is blown to hell. What's left from the wreckage?' And then they could see that I was there and be happy. I was a complete caretaker.

"This is how pitiful it was," she says, leaning back on the couch and stretching out her long legs, trying to get comfortable. "After the big house in Southampton was sold, my father rented a garage apartment at the house of some friends. Some weekends I'd go out with my friends. I'd stay in this little apartment with him, and when my friends and I went out for the evening, if Dad was alone, I'd invite him to come along because I didn't want him to be lonely. And he'd come. So there it is in a nutshell: complete caretaker, complete over-achiever, and I still flinch at the notion of being rejected."

Rachel's first husband was Curtis. "I married him because I thought he'd give me security. I ignored the fact that he was com-pletely psychotic because the abuse felt normal to me. Not that my father was abusive to me, but he was just not present.

"It's because of all this that I could stay in the marriage to Cur-tis for a long time, even though he was emotionally abusive. He often told me that I was the most selfish person in the world. Most women wouldn't stand for this, but I did. After all, I'd heard that all my life, so that made sense to me. And if my ex-husband was irra-tional, saying, 'How could you get a massage!' that made sense to me, because how could I be so selfish?

"To this day, I swear that any narcissistic person in my general vicinity is going to find me. If there were seventy-five people in the room, I would find that one sadist looking for the masochist."

Rachel remembers some good times with her father, but she also complains bitterly about her relationship with her father today: "It's not like I don't have any good memories of my father," says Rachel, trying to be fair. "I remember driving out to Southampton after work sometimes, and we'd have a good time together, and he liked to listen to music. He had good rhythm, and he'd sing and stuff. I remember a couple of real connections with him—times when I told him things and he listened.

"But today my father lives two blocks away, literally, and he has never spontaneously come to see my kids. If he sees them, it's because I call. One of the children asked me if my father hates them. I said, 'He doesn't hate you at all. He's a wreck, but you have to understand, he was a wreck before you, he was a wreck with me. He didn't show me any more affection than he does you. It's not personal.

"I think as a daughter, you always feel the disappointment. Neither of my parents called me on Christmas. And it's not even about me, but to not call their grandchildren on Christmas! And this is after my father's been going through some really bad financial stuff, and my sister and I have been incredibly supportive to him. I made this album for him of all these pictures of me in my childhood, just of me and him, to show and say, 'Look, there were these moments when we were close and you were a dad.'"

Rachel told me that one time she finally confronted her father regarding his lack of caring. "I wrote this e-mail that just spit everything out: 'You were angry when I was a child, you didn't listen, you're not listening now. You scream and you get angry when you feel anxious. But that's not what I need in my life. And where have you been? Where were you when I was getting divorced? Where have you been for my kids? When do you step up to the plate?' And when I sent him that e-mail, I knocked him down so hard that we didn't speak for I don't know how long.

"Finally I knew we had to overcome this. I went to see him, and my father sat there and was clearly devastated, but basically what he said was, 'I don't want to hear about why you wrote what you wrote. I don't want to hear what your reasons are, and I don't want you to tell me what you think of me.'

"'If all you want is to hear me say I'm sorry,' I said, 'I am sorry you're so hurt, but you know how often you hurt me? In my life?' So I got up to leave, and he said, 'If you walk out of here, we will never speak again.' So I sat down. So what can I tell you? Did it probably open some floodgates? Yeah, I think so, but at the end of the day, how capable was my father really of changing, of hearing, of listening? I'm not angry with my father. Most of the time I feel he does the best that he can. That's just not very much. I just feel so much of my father is dead. What is there to fight with?"

I asked Rachel whether her problems with her father affected her marriage to Curtis. She rolled her eyes and then said, "Absolutely. In fact, they *caused* my marriage to Curtis. That marriage was linked to the unhealthy behaviors that I developed growing up. When I married Curtis, it was as if I married my mother and my father at the same time. He represented the worst of both of them, all rolled into one man. But eventually I divorced him, and going through the divorce, I learned how strong I was. For the first time, I was able to feel who I was.

"When my current husband and I became involved romantically, even though it had its rockiness, I was able to slowly let somebody into my life in the right way. We stuck it out, and now I don't break out in hives because somebody tells me they love me or that I'm a good person. He's amazing. We're two people who are caretakers, and we finally found each other. But this couldn't have happened when I was young. I needed a great deal of experience with adult relationships in order to put into perspective the impact of my father's mental illness and my mom's narcissism on my own development.

"My life has changed in so many ways. I can see now—which is a very poignant thing—that I am actually precious to my father. I don't think that I always was. His ambition and his illness and his narcissism—all those things definitely got in the way. But I know that he's always been very proud of me, always."

Rachel clearly had a much more difficult time recovering from the effects of her father's bipolar disorder than Gail had. One reason for this is that Gail had the support of her mother, who brought stability to the household and was able to connect with her daughter. Rachel did not have this. Rachel's mom was selfish and narcissistic, and she exacerbated the impact of her father's mental illness rather than mitigated it.

In addition, Rachel's father is still alive, and Rachel is still angry with him. As she has gained perspective on her childhood and become a stronger individual with a greater capacity for healthy relationships, she still had to deal with her father. The natural result of her increasing ego strength and his continuing pathology was for her to confront him, but that only resulted in her realizing that he was still sick, and he was still incapable of meeting her needs.

The Path to Recovery

Daughters of mentally ill fathers typically experience disruptions in the normal course of development. Their homes tend to be chaotic. Fathers may be absent completely due to hospitalizations or the travels that often accompany manic episodes. Their mother, assuming she is healthy, may be preoccupied with caring for her husband or working to cover household expenses. As a result, daughters may be asked or feel compelled to take on responsibilities that are beyond their years, such as caring for younger brothers and sisters.

A daughter's experience with her mentally ill father may train her to believe that people in general or men specifically cannot be depended on for emotional support or nurturing. They may have learned to expect little from men, and they may find themselves drawn into unhealthy or abusive relationships.

Daughters of mentally ill fathers often fail to develop normal adolescent relationships with peers. They may suffer from the social stigma attached to mental illness. They may be too embarrassed to have friends over, because they fear that their father will behave in a bizarre manner that might make their friends anxious. They may be insecure regarding their own attractiveness. They may bend over backward to try to please people, and they may blame themselves for anything that goes wrong in their relationships.

Daughters of mentally ill fathers do best when they have a resilient and caring mother, significant social support from family and friends, and an understanding that the problems at home are a function of their father's mental illness. When support and insight are available during childhood and early adolescence, they tend to fare well. When they do not receive such support and insight until after they have entered young adulthood and left the home, the recovery process can be slower.

A child with a mentally ill parent needs to be told what is happening, and the well parent, assuming there is one, is naturally the one whom we would expect to perform this task. But the well parent may need help in learning how to do this. In such cases a therapist, a pastor who has had experience in counseling, or even a Web site such as www.pathways2promise.org or www.lightship.org can provide information that will help the whole family understand the onset of mental illness, the effects of medication, the grief and loss that occur when a beloved parent becomes alien, and the need to set limits on destructive and erratic behavior.

There are groups that provide support (Alliance for the Mentally Ill) and books such as *When Madness Comes Home*, by Victoria Secunda, that help to make sense of a senseless situation. (The entries in Resources for Readers at the end of the book will provide help to daughters and other family members who are trying to cope with the father's mental illness.)

If you are the daughter of a mentally ill father, you owe it to yourself to learn as much as you can about the illness. This knowledge may go a long way toward explaining why he acted as he did, and it may free you from the erroneous belief that there must have been something wrong with you. You should make this effort regardless of how old you are. Even women who think that they have long since recovered from the havoc wrought by their father's mental illness may see new ways in which it affected them and new ways in which they can work to form healthy relationships.

Chapter Three

The Substance-Abusing Father

In my clinical practice, research, and personal experience, I've found that fathers who abuse alcohol and other addictive drugs frequently manifest many of the same characteristics as fathers who are mentally ill. They are unpredictable, undependable, and embarrassing. They tend to vacillate between affection and rejection. They are often angry and sometimes verbally or physically abusive.

Daughters who grow up with substance-abusing fathers tend to experience a variety of problems when they are children. They often feel guilty, assuming that they are somehow responsible for their father's drinking. They tend to be anxious, because they never know what might happen next. They may fear that their parents will fight, or that their alcoholic father will become unpredictably abusive toward their mother or themselves.

Young daughters of alcoholic and drug-dependent fathers are frequently confused because their homes lack order. Changes in the behavior of the substance abuser disrupt routines, and the mother often devotes so much energy to coping with her husband's drinking that she cannot always compensate for the lack of structure. Because daughters of addicted fathers are completely unable to control their situations, they may feel helpless and dependent.

Adult daughters of alcoholics tend to display predictable patterns of behavior as a result of their childhood experiences. Because the homes of alcoholic fathers are often chaotic and unpredictable, women who grow up in these homes may fail to develop any understanding of what normal behavior really is. They become used to plans falling apart and projects that are begun but never taken through to completion. Accordingly, it has been observed that adult children of alcoholics themselves may find it difficult to complete tasks. The adult daughter of an alcoholic father may not even appreciate the importance of actually completing projects that she has begun. This can affect her academic and work performance.

Similarly, because alcoholic fathers frequently hide their drinking and its consequences, the adult daughter of an alcoholic may find it difficult to be honest. She may have particular difficulty recognizing and expressing negative emotional states or identifying problems with relationships. The inability to understand and work through relationship issues tends to put stress on friendships, romantic relationships, and marriages. Alcoholic households are typically tense places, where good times and fun are not the norm. For this reason, adult daughters of alcoholic fathers may have difficulty getting enjoyment out of life. They may even associate having fun with an impending cataclysm—an alcoholic can often change from Goodtime Charlie to Nasty Ned as the drinks continue to be poured and the alcohol level rises. Much has been written about the problems often experienced by adult children of alcoholics, and support groups have arisen in response to the difficulties these adults tend to experience. The same dynamics are relevant to the daughters of fathers who are addicted to other drugs. This chapter tells the stories of women who describe their fathers as substance abusers. These men came in many different forms, but in each case, it is apparent that the disease contributed to the emotional absence of the father. In some cases, the father was physically absent as well. The substance abuse of a father also tends to preoccupy the mother, rendering her less than fully available to her children.

The emotional unavailability of the substance-abusing father often leads his daughter to redouble her efforts to secure acceptance and validation from others. If she is an older child, she may assume many of the responsibilities for managing the household and caring for younger siblings. She may become a compulsive overachiever in an effort to gain approval for herself and respectability for the family. She may assume responsibility for repairing emotional damage suffered by family members, and this tendency may generalize to friends and coworkers. Efforts at winning acceptance and approval combine with efforts to "fix" everyone's problems, with the result that the daughters of substance abusers are often identified as suffering from the people-pleaser syndrome.

"I Always Felt That I Had to Be Really Nice to People"

Carey, thirty-four years old, is the assistant administrator of the only nursing home in the town where she grew up—a small, rural community in New York's Catskill Mountains. She is married to John, a thirty-two-year-old carpenter, and they have three children ranging in age from thirteen to sixteen.

Carey said that she was pregnant when she got her high school diploma and "very pregnant" when she got married that summer. She was ambivalent about getting married when she did. "John was the first and only boy I had ever dated, and I had planned on going to college." However, she said that in retrospect she couldn't really complain, because John was a good husband, a good father, and a steady provider.

Carey's father, Roger, was a stonecutter in a bluestone quarry until he died two years ago at the age of fifty. Carey's mother, Pam, works in town at the market as a cashier, a job she has had for nearly thirty years. Carey was an only child. After she was born, she said, her mom was afraid to have any more children because she knew Roger was an alcoholic, and she was insecure about their finances. Although Roger worked hard his whole life, there were many times when "the money never made it home." Often it was the money that Pam earned at the market that paid for rent and food.

Carey explained that for most of his life and the first half of her life, her father was a "weekend drinker." By that she meant that he would go to work each day and not drink more than a few beers a day during the week. However, Fridays were "party time." He would start drinking at the local bar with his buddies as soon as he got off work on Friday, and he drank more or less continuously until Sunday night. He hung out with a drinking crowd that included many of his lifelong school friends and his friends at work.

He always did seem to drink more than the rest of them, but they all drank enough that for some time, he didn't seem so bad by comparison. In fact, for a long time, the extent of his problem didn't really sink in. When he and Carey's mother were dating, it never occurred to her that he was an alcoholic. He was just another fun-loving guy. But after they had been married for a time, the problem came into sharper focus, starting the first time Roger came home at 5:00 A.M. on a Saturday morning having spent his entire paycheck.

While Carey was growing up, her father's alcoholism progressed, and the problem became clear to everyone. He spent most or all of his paycheck at the bar on many occasions, until he finally gave in to Pam's pressure to have his check deposited directly into the family bank account.

Carey remembers several occasions when her father missed parent-teacher conferences and her school plays. She remembers several occasions on which her father was drunk in public, and he embarrassed her in front of her friends. She remembers promises he made that were never kept, either because it turned out that he didn't have the money that he thought he would have to fulfill the promise or because he didn't remember making the promise. Once he didn't come home on Christmas Eve until 3:00 A.M., and he was so hung over the next day that he couldn't participate when the presents were opened.

Roger was stopped for drunk driving several times, but he never got in legal trouble, because the small town constable was a good friend of his from school. The constable would just make Roger leave his car by the side of the road, and he would give Roger a ride home. Luckily, he was never stopped by the state police. These incidents were still embarrassing to Carey, however, because the constable's daughter was in her school, and pretty soon everyone was making jokes about his drinking.

Roger began to have blackouts, and one time he called from Atlantic City to get someone to come and pick him up. He had no money, no car, and no recollection of how he had gotten there. He had been gone for three days, and no one knew where he was. The last thing he remembered on that prolonged binge was being at the bar in his home town, talking to a friend about some system the friend had developed for winning at roulette.

Pam had gone into a panic, because she assumed her husband was dead. Carey was also upset and afraid when her dad was missing, but she coped with the situation by helping her mom through it. She missed school for two days to stay at home with Pam until they found out that Roger was okay.

Carey said that her mom and dad "never stopped loving each other," despite the craziness surrounding his drinking. Her mom, she told me, was very bright and felt that her husband had a disease. Her mom was also resourceful, and she was able to keep the household together despite the stresses associated with Roger's alcoholism.

Carey felt that a part of her mother's resilience was a matter of her strong personal character, but Carey also pointed out that at a certain point, their pastor had referred her mom to ALANON and her to ALATEEN meetings that took place in a nearby town. Carey said that these support groups had been very helpful to both of them. The meetings provided a great deal of information about alcoholism and her father's behavior. The meetings also provided social support and many practical suggestions regarding how to minimize the impact of the problem

Carey also thought that on some level, her dad accepted the fact that he was an alcoholic and tried to quit drinking a few times. He was never an ugly drunk who insulted people or got into fights. He was always apologetic after he had embarrassed or disappointed Carey or her mother.

But he was nevertheless a drunk—an embarrassing, undependable drunk. And toward the end of his life, he began drinking heavily most of the time. He missed days at work because he was drunk or hung over. His health deteriorated, and he died early of liver disease.

In retrospect, Carey was very much aware of how much her dad's alcoholism had affected her life. She had been very upset when her father had failed to show up where he was expected, and she was mortified when he was obviously drunk in front of her friends. She told me that she was angry at him for making it "impossible for Mom to ever quit her job," and she was mad at him as well for forcing her "to take up the slack around the house." Carey was convinced that she did many more chores at home than most of her friends did and that she had less time for simply hanging out. This wasn't so much because her mother or her father demanded that she do these chores, she said, but rather because she felt sorry for her mother, who had to work so hard. She wanted to make the load a little lighter.

Carey also felt obligated to "be really nice to people," because she wanted to gain back the approval that she thought had been lost through her father's drinking. She said that she would do almost anything anyone wanted if she thought it would make that person like her. She thought that was the most important factor that led her to become pregnant so young. She noted as well times when she felt as if she had no control over what might happen to her and was "just at the mercy of God."

Carey had considered college and thought she had good enough grades, but college seemed to be a hopeless dream. Her family couldn't help her out financially, and she was reluctant to be any distance from her mom. When she got pregnant and John wanted to get married, she figured that was just the way God had planned things out for her. Carey and John settled down in an apartment in his parents' home, a half mile from Carey's home.

John did reasonably well as a carpenter, but Carey always tried to sandwich a little work around her kids' schedules. She did this primarily to have a little extra money for Christmas presents and other extras, but she also said that her mom had told her to always have a job of her own, just in case something happened and John couldn't work (or took up drinking). This was basically a message that a woman with a family can never depend completely on a man.

As one of her various part-time jobs, Carey took some shifts as an aide at the local nursing home. Although some folks would consider this menial work and not very rewarding, Carey really liked it. She loved interacting with the elderly residents and enjoyed talking with their relatives when they visited. She said it made her feel good to let the family members know that their elderly loved ones were getting a lot of attention and being well cared for. Carey said that in a funny way, she thought that the experience of trying to ease her mother's burdens in coping with her father's alcoholism prepared her for her work in the nursing home: it showed how "doing some little tangible things for someone not only relieves them of some of their work, but also comforts them by letting them know that someone cares."

Given Carey's strong need to nurture and her friendly manner, it is not surprising that when her children got a little older and she could consider working full time, she put in more time and energy and was promoted to a position as assistant manager of the nursing home. She and John are in the process of making quite a nice life for themselves. They are proud of their children, all of whom are "really good kids" and honor students. Carey is quite certain that they will all go to college and that she and John will be able to help them achieve this goal.

Carey experienced many of the difficulties that are typical to daughters of alcoholic fathers, and to some extent, she was rather fortunate that her life has turned out so well. She did miss out on some of the social activities that young girls have in school, and it is certainly possible that without Roger's disease in the mix, she might have gone off to college and perhaps ended up in a very different job, perhaps in a different place. Her people-pleasing orientation has had good and bad effects. It probably goes a long way toward explaining why she got pregnant so young. It probably also explains her success at the nursing home.

Carey was fortunate in that her pastor referred her mom and her to appropriate support groups. It was certainly helpful to realize that others have the same problem, that the problem was not her fault, and that there are steps that one can take in order to gain a degree of control over the situation. Carey was also fortunate that John turned out to be the reliable husband and father that he is. I believe she is also very much aware of how fortunate she has been.

"My Father Shot My Dog"

The story of Katherine is in some ways similar to that of Carey, in that their alcoholic fathers were not physically or emotionally abusive to their wives or their daughters. They just behaved like the drunks that they were, with the result that they were embarrassing, unpredictable, and undependable. The two stories are similar as well in that neither of the fathers in question disappeared or wound up in jail, which is not often the case with substance-abusing fathers.

One dramatic difference between the two stories, however, is that Katherine's father had inherited a share of an immense family fortune and was extremely wealthy. The wealth eliminated the issue of the constant threat of financial insecurity that Carey's family had to deal with. Katherine was not held back in her education or career aspirations by her father's alcoholism, and she became a successful sculptor. But her social adjustment was clearly affected, and in this regard, she was not as lucky as Carey, at least not the first time around.

"I grew up in Minneapolis, Minnesota, in a lovely house on the lake," says Katherine, a woman in her seventies with a fragile beauty that belies her age. "I had an extraordinarily beautiful mother and a father who was also very handsome in his way, and elegant. He'd gone to Princeton and was a friend of F. Scott Fitzgerald, and he made beautiful mint juleps served in frosted glasses for people playing tennis on Sundays. It's what I remember from my childhood—very Old World, very WASP. Golf, tennis, playing— that kind of thing."

Her father's family owned a large timber company, and Katherine can remember being taken to the sawmills as a child and how thrilling it was to see the men jumping from log to log as they floated them down the river to the mill. Being there made her feel proud of her father, she remembers. But when her father turned forty, he sold his interest to cousins and retired to a life of fishing, hunting, golfing—and drinking.

He was extremely accomplished at these activities, Katherine told me: "He was a world-class fisherman. He was a world-class shotgunner. He was a world-class golfer. I mean world class. To watch him cast a fly was one of the most beautiful things in the world, or to swing a golf club. I see a great athlete, and I think of my father, because my father was coordinated in that same lyrical way. And he had friends with whom he shared these activities, and they all loved him. But they were probably all alcoholics as well.

"As a child I didn't know about alcoholism. I just knew that my father started acting strangely around dinner, that sometimes at the dinner table he would be very gruff or very suspicious. And when he and my mother had parties, he would sing. As a child I was so embarrassed, I could hardly stand it. He would lie on the floor, drunk, in front of everyone and sing his favorite song, "O Sole Mio," and mother always looked embarrassed and humiliated.

"They got divorced when I was about eleven. Mother went roaring off to Lake Forest, Illinois, but my brother and I were sent back to Minneapolis every year to spend the summer with Daddy. By that time he was *really* drinking. When we were with him, he would go out every night drinking. He didn't spend any time with us. He didn't even arrange for a babysitter or a companion to spend the evenings with us. It was like he was so into his socializing and his drinking that it never occurred to him that he was also a father and needed to act like one.

"So every night, he would go out in his Mercury convertible down the long, long, long, looong driveway, and when he came back, he would be really drunk. I used to stay awake until he got back, because I was worried that he was going to kill himself driving drunk. Finally, I would hear the car or see the lights weaving down the driveway. Pretty soon he would tiptoe into my room quietly and lean over to be sure I was asleep. The only problem was that his tip-toeing was more like staggering, so even if I hadn't been awake already when he drove down the driveway, I woke up when he came to see if I was sleeping. I would breathe in very deeply so that he would think I was asleep. I was actually terrified that he would realize that I wasn't sleeping. And then he'd do the same thing with my brother.

"It wasn't that I was afraid he was going to hurt me, because he never did raise a hand to me, although he did have a quick temper when he was drunk. No, it was more like I was afraid that if he knew I was awake, he'd say, 'What are you doing? Why are you awake? You're supposed to be asleep.' And if he had said something gruff like that, I would have been afraid, because I didn't feel as if I really knew him.

"My father was never soothing or loving. I don't remember his hugging me or holding me or even touching me in any way. I always felt ill at ease with him. He was charming and sociable when he was around his fishing and golfing buddies. He was the life of the party at the hunting lodge. But he didn't know how to relate to his children. And most of the time when my brother and I spent summers with him, we were very lonely. That changed just a bit when he remarried. The new marriage didn't change him or his alcoholism, but my father's second wife was very nice to me and my brother, so at least after she came into the picture, we didn't feel so lonely.

"When I was twelve, my father shot my dog. It was an accident because he was drunk and cleaning his guns. And he had to come and tell me that he'd killed my labrador. He called me into his room with tears in his eyes and said, 'Katherine, what you have to understand is I have a disease, and I'm sick, and the disease is alcohol. And I am so, so sorry. Please forgive me.'

"That's the only time I ever heard him remorseful. I said, 'Oh, Daddy, that's okay,' but of course it wasn't okay. I was very, very angry with him, but I was afraid to let it out.

"We did have some good times with him, however, right after he got married again. The best fun I ever had with him, though he didn't do it for us, was when we were out West on one of our camping trips. He used to take my brother and me and his new wife to these marvelous places in Idaho. I remember watching him cast a fly and thinking how beautiful it was. That was really one of the happiest times of my life.

"One night when we were out West, he got very drunk and decided he was going to cook dinner. He went into the cupboard in the cabin and opened every single can there was—every single one—and put it all into a gigantic black kettle and boiled it up, and that's what we had for dinner. I think it was chili and tomatoes and sausages and beans and—I don't know what. Anyway, it was all dropped in, because he was so drunk. He would stir, and then another can went in, and he would stir it some more. It was the consistency and color of dog food, but oddly enough, it was very good."

One thing that seems certain is that Katherine didn't learn from her father's example what kind of man a women should seek out as a husband. In fact, it seems that she learned just the opposite, for her first husband was very much like her father, alcoholism and all.

At one point in our interview, Katherine remarked, "I hated my father and loved him at the same time, and with my first husband, I think tried to marry him."

Katherine's first husband, Jack, was the son of one of her father's wealthy sportsman drinking companions. He was very much like his father and very much like Katherine's father. He was handsome and could cast a fly like her father. Katherine also pointed out that they came from similar backgrounds and had some similar interests, but it is the similarity to her father that stands out. They had two children together, but the marriage didn't last. Her husband's drinking became even more embarrassing than her father's had been, and her husband was downright nasty to her and their children when he had been drinking a lot.

Eventually Katherine began to feel ill at ease around him even when he was not drinking, and she sometimes found herself fearful that he might harm her or the children when he was drinking. With the support of a couple of friends who counseled her to get out, she filed for divorce, a step that she sees as the "beginning of her liberation from her father's tyranny."

The divorce also freed her to reengage socially and to meet her second husband—the man whom Katherine regards as helping her "find herself" again. Interestingly, this second husband also shared some qualities with her father, but this time the similarity was not the alcoholic part of her father or the sporting adventuresome part of her father, but rather the brilliant intellectual part.

"He was the most influential person in my life, the most brilliant, intellectual, funniest, skeptical, unboring man I've ever known. He had read everything, he remembered everything; he taught me about Henry James, about Edith Wharton, about Cafavy, the poet, about history, about politics. He had this enormous mind, and he taught me so much. He really educated me in a way that nobody else could have, because he was not just smart; he was *interested*. He supported my work as a sculptor. He understood that it mattered, and he gave me the freedom to do it. He died two years ago. I miss him terribly, but my relationship with him made me whole again."

With Katherine, we note first and foremost that she acknowledged herself that she didn't know much about alcoholism. In this regard, Carey had an advantage over her, because it seems doubtful that Katherine would have married her first husband if she had had better knowledge of alcoholism when she met him. At any rate, Katherine was not as lucky as Carey in her initial choice of husbands. Katherine benefited from the support of friends in mustering up the courage to divorce. Katherine finally found a mutually supportive relationship with her second husband, and it was through the validation she received from him that she was able to find herself.

"Sixties Party Dad with Money"

The word people use to describe Betsy, now almost forty years old, is *cute*, probably because she's a small, finely boned woman with a mop of flyaway blonde hair. But behind the fragile, childlike exterior is a divorced woman raising two small children and working as a child psychiatrist. Her career path is amazing given Betsy's stories of her disastrous adolescence and early academic failures. She describes her father as a wealthy alcoholic who spent his life partying, and she describes her mother as a nonentity who deferred to her father in every area, even after they divorced, simply because her father was the source of the money that continued to support her lifestyle.

"I have two memories of my dad from the time before my parents were divorced, which was when I was seven. I remember him cooking a hot dog on the grill outside on our terrace and thinking it was odd, because he never did that. And I remember going into his bedroom one weekend morning, and when I woke him up, I said to him, 'You smell like a hangover.' Those are the only two memories from back then. I don't think I spent any time with him at all. Mostly he wasn't home. It was always just my mom.

"He wasn't mean or anything like that. He just was not around. I found out later that most of the time, he was simply off running his own life, which involved managing family money, doing a lot of drinking and drugging, and having many, many brief affairs. A friend once referred to him as a 'sixties party dad with money.'

"Before my parents divorced, it seemed like my mom was pretty much oblivious to my father's comings and goings. He paid the bills reliably, and she seemed pretty much content with the situation. She had affairs as well, although she was never into partying and drugs in quite the same manner as my dad, and she was much more discrete about her lovers. I think they divorced pretty much out of mutual convenience. Dad made it clear that he would continue to support all of us, and that suited Mom. They didn't fight. Mom's job was to take care of us on a day-to-day basis, and Dad's job was to finance the deal.

"My parents were divorced when I was seven, and my father moved to St. Louis. My brother and I didn't see him for a year, though occasionally we'd talk on the phone. Then he moved back to Chicago, and every two weeks, he'd drive out to Winnetka to pick us up, and we'd stay with him for the weekend. My brother would sit in the front, and I would always be in the back, leaning forward between the front bucket seats. My dad would have a six-pack of Budweiser in the back and he'd say, 'Kitcat, give me a beer.' That was my role: to hand him his beer while he was driving. And then he'd smoke Marlboro cigarettes with the window cracked.

"That period is really the beginning of my clear memories of him, because from then on, we saw him regularly. We'd go to a movie or a show or out to dinner. I looked forward to it because we'd get to sleep on the floor of his apartment in sleeping bags—he had only one bedroom—and we'd go out to dinner at this French restaurant on the Near North Side and the maître d' would fawn over me because I was so young. It made me feel great. I'd always have the same thing: duck à l'orange and chocolate mousse.

"My father always brought along a date when we'd go out to eat, and afterward we'd all go back to the apartment, and whoever he was with would stay over. And that was weird, of course. The women would usually last for a couple of dates; then there'd be a new one.

"In the summer, he'd rent a place on the lake and invite friends for the weekend. I guess I was about ten by then, and I was the one responsible for pouring and serving the drinks. He also made me the person in charge of guests. He'd say, 'Get this room ready for so-and-so.' And he and his friends would be smoking pot and things like that. But everyone was always very nice. Never any inappropriate comments or gestures or anything like that."

When I suggested that her father had no idea how to be a parent, Betsy nodded her head in agreement. "Exactly. Being a parent was my mother's role. With my father, it was hanging out and partying. Every once in a while, he'd try to act like a parent, but he was really inconsistent. I remember the first time I ever had a drink with him at a bar. I was a freshman in high school, fourteen years old, and I had brought my friend Eva with me for the weekend. She was really attractive, superprecocious, a wickedly funny girl. And she and my father were openly flirting with one another. I mean, openly. That was a really bizarre interaction. But from then on, my father, my brother, and I would all go out drinking together. Then later we smoked pot together and even went on an LSD trip.

"From my early teens, that was my relationship with my father. He treated me like an adult more than a child. He'd given me a credit card, and almost every month there'd be this freak-out about what I had spent. But he never gave me a boundary, telling me how much I could spend or what I could buy. So when he got the bill each month, he would freak out about it and threaten to take my card away. But he never did.

"I remember alternating between thinking he was this really cool dad and then thinking he was a total asshole. And I don't know whether it was adolescent acting-out behavior or simply behavior modeled on what I saw with dear old Dad, but when I was in prep school, I was wasted most of the time. I never studied, and I was a real slut—an überslut. I was thrown out of my first prep school for using drugs. I managed to finish high school at a second prep school, and I got into college. In college, I continued to drink and drug, sleep around, and perform miserably academically. I nearly flunked out freshman year, but then I sort of mellowed out and did a little bit better, and I got my bachelor's degree in psychology. Later on, I finally got my shit together and decided that I wanted to go to medical school. I had to go back to a two-year postbaccalaureate program so that I could meet the requirements and get some good grades. And even then I had to go to medical school in the Virgin Islands.

"My parents were aware that I was running off the deep end during high school and college. They just didn't seem to care about it. At least they didn't care about it very much. I remember when I almost flunked out of college my first semester, my dad told me, 'I don't care what kind of grades you get. I'm just paying the bills.'

"And I remember how my mother reacted to my promiscuity when I was in high school. I remember how one time she was driving me back to school when I was sixteen, and she said, 'I just want you to know that if you ever get into trouble you can talk to me,' meaning like if I was to get pregnant. It didn't occur to them that my sleeping around wasn't just about sex. Now I realize that I was trying to find someone to love me, hoping the sex would develop into some kind of relationship."

Betsy is not completely clear as to what it was that led her to turn her life around, but she did mention a number of factors that may have played a role. I alluded to her use of the term "mellowed out" to describe a gradual shift that took place after around her first year in college. She mentioned that she remained at school over the summer after her freshman year, and I got the feeling that in college, Betsy began to become a little bit more independent and less compelled to act out in order to try to get her parents' attention.

When she was graduated from college, she moved to the West Coast along with two friends from college. She got a job in a day care center and found she had an interest in working with children. She dated a medical student and seemed to benefit from the exposure to his work ethic and sense of purpose. She became more health conscious, and she lost interest in doing drugs entirely.

For two years, she saw her parents only once a year each, at Christmas. She took a graduate-level course in child psychology and did well. Then she took a course in neuropsychology. Although her dating relationship with the medical student did not progress, they remained friends, and he encouraged her to think about medical school. More than two years after completing college, Betsy wrote to her father to ask if he would pay for her to go back to school for a two-year postbaccalaureate premedical program. He agreed without hesitation, but without any great display of pride or elation either. If that's what she wanted, he didn't mind helping out. From that point on, Betsy did well in school and steadily progressed toward her goal of becoming a child psychiatrist.

Six years later, Betsy moved to New York City to complete her psychiatry residency. There, at the age of thirty, she met her first husband, Jack. "When I met Jack, I knew he was moving to Scotland to become involved with family business there, which involved the manufacturing and international marketing of Scottish woolen garments. So I was thinking it would be a brief summer fling. But Jack came back to the States, and he asked if he could stay with me while he looked for a place. I said sure. Then once we'd been living together for a while, people started asking when we were getting married. I thought, 'Well, I'm thirty and I want to have kids,' and he was there. So we got married.

"Jack was like my dad in some ways. Although he wasn't into drugs or alcohol the way my dad was, Jack liked to party, and he felt that he was entitled to have things given to him. Within two years after we married, he quit his full-time job as a manager in a New York–based importing company. He continued to dabble in a few ventures, mostly connected to the family business back home. But mostly he just hung out.

"I went along with it, because it made me feel in control. We had two children in relatively short order, and Jack was very good with them. He became basically a stay-at-home dad, although he never gave up working on one project or another. However, after seven years, I really grew tired of his lack of purpose, and I asked for a divorce. He wasn't surprised by the request, and he agreed to the split. Since then, he has gone back and forth between the States and Scotland. I have physical custody of the kids, but he is very much involved with them as well."

And now there is a new man in Betsy's life. The new man, Wallace, is different. He is a caretaker-protector kind of guy. He is also a psychiatrist—a man who views his own life as having a purpose and meaning. He is a few years older than Betsy. She describes him as successful, dependable, and loving. She loves to discuss their clinical work with him, and, she said, their discussions reinforce the idea that she has made something of her life and the reassuring notion that she is contributing to society. She also said that for the first time in her life, she feels that she has a partner.

Betsy's early drugging and promiscuity was aimed primarily at getting her father to sit up and take notice or her. It was as if she was screaming to her father, "Look up from your glass and take notice of me. Can't you see I need a father?"

But Betsy's dad couldn't see beyond his glass or the smoke rising from his joint. He was so laid back that he didn't even recognize that she was crying out for his help. In order for her to recover from his failure as a father, Betsy had to first gain enough distance from his pathology that she could begin to see herself as an independent actor in the world. This seems to have begun after her freshman year in college.

At that point, she had to make up for lost time finding where she fit into that world. This occurred gradually, through her experience working in a day care center and new friends who made her see both joys and advantages associated with not being stoned all the time. The encouragement of a friend with ambition gave Betsy the idea that maybe she could accomplish more academically, and fortunately Betsy's laissez-faire father had sufficient resources that he could afford to finance her postbaccalaureate and medical school expenses.

Even after Betsy had become an adult working professional, vestiges of her father's failure to overcome remained. Betsy's choice of a first husband was not well thought through. It was not a nightmare, but it had little chance of developing into a mutually satisfying life partnership. This has only come about with her current relationship.

The Path to Recovery

These interviews with women whose unavailable fathers failed them through substance abuse reveal several of the characteristic responses of children to parental addiction. Carey reacted to her father's alcoholism by becoming a people pleaser. She sought to overcome the embarrassment her father regularly brought on the family by being the best child and the best friend that she could be. And for Carey, things worked out fairly well. She may well have closed some doors for her future when she became pregnant at such an early age, but she was fortunate in several important areas. She and her mom were referred to support groups that helped them understand alcoholism and how to minimize the havoc it wrought. In addition, her young husband proved to be solid as a rock. She also lucked out by falling into the nursing home work where her people-pleasing skills were valued and rewarded.

Katherine's response to her dashing alcoholic father was to alternate between hating him for not being a father and loving him for being the handsome, mythic sportsman that he was. Unfortunately for Katherine, she needed to marry a carbon copy of her dad before she figured out that he was not a model of the ideal life partner. It required the thoughtful intervention of some friends to set her thinking straight on what she needed, but she eventually rid herself of the first husband, the remnant of her father's failure to parent, and she ultimately found a more appropriate partner.

Betsy illustrates the lengths to which children of substance-abusing parents will go to try to get the attention and the parenting that they require and want. Betsy tried out all the standard adolescent rebellious acting-out behaviors that she could come up with on the basis of her life experience. She screwed up at school, took every drug that she could lay her hands on, and engaged in premature and promiscuous sexual activity. The only problem with Betsy's acting out was that none of these behaviors really bothered her father that much, because he, after all, was also participating in most of them himself. So Betsy couldn't really separate from him through drugs and sex. She required time and distance, exposure to a different set of values, and eventually the support of new friends to find out who she was and could be.

Chapter Four

The Abusive Father

Childhood abuse of daughters by their fathers takes many forms. Of course, in one sense, all the fathers we have discussed thus far could be viewed as abusive. Disapproving fathers are abusive in the sense that they fail to validate their daughters' existence and self-worth. Mentally ill fathers and substance-abusing fathers are abusive in that they fail to provide the orderly and predictable home environment that their daughters need to feel secure and confident in their interactions with the world. Many children take on the "burden of badness" because it's easier to see themselves as bad rather than the parent. There is no hope if the parent and his or her world is bad, but if children blame themselves, there is still hope that they can change to improve things, and all hope is not lost.

But the abusive fathers in the stories in this chapter are different. These fathers have not just failed to provide something that their daughters needed. Rather, they have engaged in active behaviors that are harmful to their daughters. These are fathers who have attacked their daughters. These attacks may be verbal, physical, or sexual in nature. Regardless of the form of the attack, the intent is to inflict harm.

And these attacks do inflict harm. Regardless of the form, the attacks are traumatic, and the effects are both immediate and long term. As children and adolescents, abused daughters tend to be anxious, fearful, and phobic. They are often angry, depressed, or socially withdrawn. They tend to be disruptive in school, and they often deliver poor academic performance.

As adults, these daughters tend to suffer from a broad range of psychosocial adjustment difficulties, including the inability to establish close relationships, sexual dysfunction, eating and substance abuse disorders, self-destructive thoughts and behavior, and posttraumatic stress disorder. The women who tell their stories in this chapter illustrate many of these negative adult outcomes among women who have been abused emotionally, physically, and or sexually by their fathers or stepfathers.

"Shutting Out the Insults"

Margaret is a sixty-one-year-old attorney who has been married and divorced five times. She has two grown children from her first marriage. She works for a large New York City firm, and her job is to supervise its pro bono work. This work brings her into contact with individuals who are quite different from the clients of the typical New York lawyer. She works with people who are often poor, angry, and incarcerated. She indicated to me that she likes her work very much, because "I feel like I have an opportunity to save people." I also had the impression that Margaret enjoys this work because these clients look up to her and she receives heartfelt thanks and a great deal of praise from them.

Margaret recognizes and freely admits that she has "intimacy issues." Although she was married five times, she told me that she was never really very close to any of her husbands. One marriage lasted only five days. The longest lasted eleven years. Of the husband who lasted the longest, Margaret said, "He was a great husband, but he wanted to have children, and I already had two and I didn't want to have his child." It appears that because of this issue of children, Margaret was able to walk away from this lengthy relationship with scarcely a second thought.

Perhaps the best indication of Margaret's inability to form close attachments is this incident that she related to me.

"My mother called me on the phone and told me that Barry Curtis had died.

"I asked her, 'Who is Barry Curtis?'

"She said, 'Your first husband, you idiot.'"

At first I was certain that Margaret had made up this story. It was incredible to me that a woman could forget the name of a man to whom she had been married. By the conclusion of our interview, however, I was completely convinced that Margaret was indeed capable of forgetting or blocking out an ex-husband's name. She is a woman who has never allowed herself to get emotionally close to a man. She has never allowed herself to "need" a man. She had fought against such attachments because she is afraid of getting hurt.

Margaret's father was a physician who worked in the military. She describes him as rigid, controlling, and verbally abusive to both her and her younger sister. At home, "He had all these rules that we had to follow. No chocolate in the house; no white bread; no loud music. We had to be up at a certain time and in bed at a certain time. We couldn't have friends from school over to visit us at the house, and we were rarely allowed to attend social events at other kids' homes. Television was permitted for only one hour each day, from 6:00 to 7:00 each evening. There were no exceptions with respect to the 'one hour only' rule, and no changes in the time when the television could be on. If something that was important to us came on at a different time, we missed it. It didn't matter how important it was or whether the other kids at school would be watching. We missed it.

"My father inspected our rooms to make sure that they were neat and clean. And God forbid you should leave something messy or get caught with a contraband piece of candy. Then all hell would break loose. He would shout and scream like a drill sergeant yelling at his recruits. He would call us names like "swine" and "vermin." He would say that if he didn't know better, he would be certain that we could not be his daughters, since we were so stupid that we couldn't see that the rules we were given were for our own good.

"And my sister, Jennifer, got it even worse than I did, because she was a little on the chubby side. I can remember him walking into the kitchen in the morning and screaming at Jennifer and my mom that she was fat and ranting that she shouldn't eat this and she shouldn't eat that. And Jennifer would start to cry, and she would end up sobbing hysterically and hiding behind my mom as if my father's words were like knives or arrows that she had to dodge. Sometimes my mother would try to stop these verbal attacks by pointing out to him that they were traumatizing Jennifer, but that would just make things worse.

"He would scream at my mother, 'Go back to your bedroom. Your daughter is fat. Leave me with my daughter.' Meaning only me. Not my poor sister. And I remember all this happening when Jennifer was maybe only five years old."

Margaret was clearly stressed by her father's anger—both the anger he directed toward her and the angry insults toward her sister that she witnessed. Margaret told me that to help her cope with her father's insults and angry diatribes, she had developed a habit of closing her eyes whenever something bad occurred. She said that she was hoping that she could "blink it away." "It's a blinking away thing," she explained. "I do it physically, and my brain is so accustomed to knowing that when I do that, it's time to shut down that it works. I blink and the memory is gone. At least for that moment."

Physically turning away from aversive events or attempting to remove them from one's consciousness is a classic response to experienced or witnessed trauma. It's like when people close their eyes and turn their heads during the most gruesome parts of a horror movie. Margaret told me that to this day, she still closes her eyes whenever she sees a person who is angry or abusive, in either real life or on television.

Margaret's father was controlling and abusive right up until the time that Margaret was able to get out on her own. She told me that when she went away to college, she lived in a dormitory with no phones in the rooms. There were only pay phones outside the building. And her father insisted that she go outside and stand at the pay phone each morning at 8:00 A.M. in order to receive a phone call from him. He insisted on making these calls because he didn't trust her to get up each morning and go off to class. And he told her that if he should call one morning and she was not there, he would come to the school and bring her back.

I commented that Margaret must have done well in college, since she had attended law school and now worked for a well-known New York law firm. She explained that she had been highly motivated to make something of herself, because she viewed academic and vocational success as a means through which she could escape from her father's control and abuse. She said she loved her law career because "it took me completely away from a reality that I didn't want to be around. My law career made me independent. And it also gave me a sense of being connected to something. I never got that from my family, and I have always wanted it. I have never gotten it from men—from any of my husbands—but I have gotten a taste of it in my work.

"Once when I was young, I saw this building that was an orphanage and I thought, 'That would be a nice place to be. All the kids are playing together.' Yes, I really envied the kids who lived in the orphanage. At least they could play. At least they could be themselves and not have to worry about someone screaming at them and telling them how bad they were all the time.

"Well, obviously I never felt as if I could play with my sister at home, and my father was so strict that I couldn't ever have any friends from school or from the neighborhood when I was small. So the law firm has come as close as I have ever gotten to having friends to whom I feel connected. We're all there together, working long hours and sharing what we do. And my clients are my community too. In my work and my children, I have what I missed as a child."

Clearly Margaret's angry and verbally abusive father left scars that affect her to this day. She has what psychologists call an attachment disorder, which essentially means that she is afraid to get close to people. She is especially afraid to allow herself to get close to anyone who could become really significant to her—like a husband. She is less threatened by her professional relationships, and still less threatened by her clients. With the clients, she can be in control. If one were to get angry and yell at her, she could simply leave and not go back, with no harm done to her.

Margaret has gone as far as she can to obtain some gratification in the context of interpersonal relationships, but she remains incapable of opening herself up and allowing herself to become vulnerable.

"Sometimes I Still Feel His Ugly Energy"

Katie is a petite, blonde, attractive fifty-three-year-old. She is a successful editor at a major publishing house.

Katie was married for ten years during her late twenties and early thirties. She had two children with this husband, whom she describes as "darling." She describes her children as "wonderful," and she describes her current relationship with their father as "great." She suggested that they divorced while "going through a rough patch," and she speculated that if they had been able to "stick it out" then, they would probably still be married.

Katie described a loving father who was "forced out of my life" by her mother when Katie was about four years old. She also described a hateful stepfather who was physically abusive toward her, her mother, and her older sister for fourteen years, until her mother finally threw him out following a particularly vicious attack.

Katie's parents were divorced when she was eighteen months old, but she still has vivid memories of those early years with her father. A big man—six feet, two inches—and a handsome one, he would arrive to claim the weekends he'd been allotted with his two daughters. He would appear at the door wearing a starched white shirt under a brown vest, securing his two little girls into the back seat of his Cadillac, where they would find rolls of Lifesavers, packs of gum, and tiny candies.

"Always," Katie remembers. "He was very consistent."

Then they would stop at his apartment where "there would be little cowboy boots for us to wear and cowboy hats. He would have the saddles and bridles waiting for us, and we'd go off on our weekend trail ride. I've been on a horse since I was two," says Katie, remembering those days in the Texas countryside. "I was always the youngest one, the little one in the back of the line. I remember having dust from the horses in front of me in my face from the dry Texas summer. When I was around my father, I always felt an enormous amount of love. He clearly adored us. He was very much present, focused on our well-being, happiness, and safety."

When she was four, Katie's mother remarried. "I saw my father one more time as a child. I remember vividly his knocking on the door, and when the door opened I flew into his arms, wrapping my legs and arms around him. When he sat down, I snuggled into his lap." Then came her mother's hostile voice, calling her into the kitchen. "All she said was, 'Get off his lap.' Her voice was so loud that my father could hear it as well. I walked back into the living room and sat on the couch with my head down.

"I remember making eye contact with my father once. It was a look that said I knew and he knew exactly where everything was. He got up, kissed my head, and said, 'Goodbye, honey.' He never came back."

Although it would be thirty-three years before Katie saw her father again, she insists that she "never felt like he left me. I knew he adored every moment of me, as I did of him. He did not leave. He was pushed out."

Katie's new stepfather was from New Hampshire. Jack had been educated in England. A respected sportsman—a gifted tennis player, golfer, and outdoorsman—he had used his charm and connections to establish a real estate development company that was quite profitable for a period of time. Katie describes the way their lives changed after the marriage: "Suddenly my sister and I, with Jack and my mother, were visiting beautiful houses and sailing on yachts. We rode horses, wore our dirndls when we were skiing, played tennis, and knew how to navigate the waters around Galveston." At first, Katie remembers, it was all great fun, but at the same time, something was not quite right, because she and her sister always felt vaguely uncomfortable when they were around their stepfather.

"He never made eye contact with us. He never touched us unless people were taking pictures. Then he'd grab us by the shoulders and pull us in tight. 'Aren't these great girls?' As soon as the camera was gone, he'd shove us away. He was never affectionate, and he never spoke to either one of us—ever.

"Jack—my stepfather—had endless rules, and he enforced them with frightening, violent displays of anger. For example, one of his rules was, absolutely no eating in between meals, ever. But we sometimes got hungry and broke the rule. We used to take food from the refrigerator and hide in our bedrooms to eat it. Well, if he saw one of us take food out of the kitchen to the bedroom, he would kick the door in—literally.

"And you just knew that if he caught you, he was capable of beating the shit out of you. I'd always run into another room—a safe place with a strong door and lock that I knew he couldn't kick in. He could kick in the door to my sister's bedroom, but by the time he did, she'd have run out the door from her bedroom into the garden, and she'd keep running. She could stand up to him to a point, but when he got angry, she'd have to run. He went after her many times, but he never caught her. I knew he could outrun me, so I never ran. I hid in that room that had the strong locked door.

"Late at night I'd hear my mother sob and ask him, 'Why do you do these things to the girls?' He'd never answer. Once, when I was eight years old, I reached up to push away a lock of hair that had come down over his eyes. He made a fist and smacked the back of my hand hard really hard. He whacked me out of the way and said, 'Don't ever touch me.' I always felt my life was in danger.

"When I was in first or second grade, I had three friends come to play. We were in my room when he came out of nowhere, grabbed my ear, twisted it, and dragged me down the hallway to the living room. He told my friends to come with us, and when we reached the living room, he dragged me to where I'd left a pair of shoes, ground my face down into them, and said, 'Don't you ever leave your shoes in the living room again. Get up and take them to your room!' We all went back to my room and then, one by one, my friends said, 'I think I'm going to go home,' and they all left. I never had a friend in the house again.

"My sister and I were terrorized by him. At dinner he'd have a stick under the table, and if either of us put an elbow on the table or did one thing out of line, we'd get it in the shins. We were too terrified to speak during those tense dinners. He was completely jealous of my mother's attentions to us. I actually think he loved my mother, but he felt he was competing with us for my mother's love. What he felt for us was pure, unadulterated jealousy and hatred.

"My mother was a loving person, always baking cookies and taking us for walks and camping in the summer, and trying to do wonderful, creative things together. She sewed most of our clothes and had a beautiful garden. What's more, she became the sole economic support of the family. After his real estate development business ran its course, Jack was pretty useless as a breadwinner. He always had 'projects,' but he never made any money.

"Mom kept hoping Jack would get better, but he just got worse. When Jack's children from an earlier marriage came to visit in the summer, Jack was very affectionate with them. When they visited, he always kissed them goodnight. I liked them and am still in touch with them. His anger was targeted only at my sister and me.

"My mother did try to protect us by buying us a horse and keeping it in a pasture thirty minutes away. She'd have us get up early in the morning, and she'd drive us to the pasture. Then she'd pick us up as dusk settled in. She worked it out that so that we'd hardly ever be home with Jack.

"In all those years with Jack, I never experienced any kindness or tenderness—only anger, threats, and violent behavior of various types.

"I remember being very careful not to do anything that would create stress or turmoil. I was a very good girl. I was the pleaser, but my sister was different. I remember once when I had eaten granola at eleven in the morning instead of waiting for mealtime, Jack went ballistic. He was screaming about how I was 'wasting' food. This time my sister couldn't take it. She said, 'You want to see waste? Well, here it is.' Then she picked up the ten-pound bag of granola and dumped the entire thing onto the dining room floor.

"I bolted for the closet, which had a lock. My sister took off like an Olympian. My mother got out the broom and sobbed. I knew things had changed. My sister had found the strength to turn on him."

During her early teen years, Katie had gotten out of the house by acting in amateur theater productions, even getting an equity card when she was fifteen. Both she and her sister also escaped the impossible situation at home with part-time jobs.

"We worked all the time, every Thanksgiving, every Christmas, every Easter. I knew I had to succeed. There were no options. No one was going to pay for my college education. Nobody was going to buy me clothes. Nobody was going to do anything like that. I knew there was no money in our house. Money to put food on the dinner table, yes, and I never felt poor, but I knew that I had to make my own way. I was ambitious, willing to take risks, to make a fool of myself. One of the first things I did was audition for a musical at my high school. Someone else got the part, and I was very disappointed. And then the next night, they called up and said, 'Yeah, we read the wrong name. You got it.'"

Katie spent her four years in high school performing onstage in school productions and for the local Shakespeare Company. She says the training she received was invaluable: "You're going onto a big stage in front of hundreds of people. It doesn't matter whether you're the star or only a bit part. You learn how to be on stage, when to show up. The discipline of theater is very good. It's the ultimate experience of being a team player.

"When I was eighteen years old, my sister and I were home together on New Year's Eve, and we started exchanging stories of the things Jack had done to us. He and my mother had been out at a party, and by the time they got home, we were both in a rage about the way he'd abused us, though never was it sexual. Jack came through the door, clearly drunk, which was a rare occurrence, and he said, 'Your mother's sitting in the car.' Then he walked into the kitchen, got the keys to the other car, and went back outside, past the car where my mother was still sitting, crying. He got into the second car, backed it up really fast down the street, and then drove it back toward the house as fast as he could, smashing it into my mother's car.

"My sister and I watched in horror, and then she opened the car door and grabbed Mom by the arm and pulled her out. Mom wasn't hurt, but she was badly shaken. We walked her into the house, and

Jack followed us. In the kitchen my mother was still sobbing. Jack grabbed her wrist, the first time I'd ever seen him do anything like that to her. I remember slapping him on the arm, saying, 'Let her go!'

"He did, but then he turned to me and said calmly, 'I've always wanted to kill you, and now I'm going to do it.'

"He began slugging me on the head with his fists. I've always been a good athlete, so I fell to the floor, put my arms and hands over my head, and started rolling. I rolled out of the kitchen while he continued to pound away at my head, my shoulders, and my back. You can't imagine how fast this happened. I managed to get out of the kitchen, through the dining room, and into the living room with my mother screaming at the top of her lungs, 'You're hitting my child!'

"My sister finally managed to dig her fingernails into his eyeballs and that got him off me. Then she ran to the phone and started to dial 911. I got up and tried to reassure my mother. 'I'm okay.' You know. Let's not make a scene. By then my mother was screaming at Jack, 'Get out, get out!'

"He left, and my sister and I tried to comfort my mother, who was sobbing. Mom said, 'I'm going to leave him.' I remember my sister saying, 'Oh, what the hell, Mom. We're old enough to move out. You might as well stay. He's not going to affect us anymore.'

"The next day I was in the bathroom, standing at the sink with the door open, when I saw Jack. He walked by and under his breath said, 'Sorry about that,' and kept going. It was the only apology he'd ever given me.

"Later he came back to the house and took every painting, every piece of furniture, everything he could get his hands on. He took them out of the house and left. He moved in with a very rich woman, eventually marrying her, and that was the end of Jack. He was, thankfully, out of our lives forever."

After Jack left, Katie appears to have been relatively well adjusted. She went to college, supporting herself as an actress. She met an older actress who became her mentor and helped her find work. She had a relationship with a young man whom she described as "loving and supportive." Then she had a two-year affair with an older man who was a successful entertainer. Next she met the father of her two children, whom she divorced, but with whom she now has a good relationship.

When I asked Katie how it was that she seems to have come through her long experience with Jack's physical abuse and emerge relatively whole, she laughed. She explained that she had mulled that over a lot, and she thought that she and her sister were helped by the fact that their mother was a buffer and that they felt that they had to protect her, just as she felt that she had to protect them. She also said that having her sister helped a lot, because it made her realize that Jack's abusiveness had nothing to do with any flaw in her. He was just a miserable, angry man.

Finally, Katie said that she always remembered that her dad had loved her, and this made her realize that she did not deserve the treatment she received from Jack. Later in her life, she reconnected with her father and confirmed her impression that he had been driven away by her mother when Jack came onto the scene.

"For me the critical thing was that I got in touch with my father. I found him. The five-year-old who lives inside me knew that I was loved by him. And I also knew that he was a flawed, fragile person. I knew that my mother was a wonderful, powerful, completely dominant woman. And I could see how she could crush him, like a bug. And so it was not complicated for me to understand that he could not take her on. But I honest to God never felt like he wasn't there because he didn't want to be. I felt like he wasn't there because he couldn't be."

However, Katie also said that she had not emerged completely untouched by her experiences with Jack. Sometime after her divorce, she had a two-year relationship with a new man who was not good for her at all—a man who was in many ways quite like her stepfather: "In my late forties I spent a few years seeing a man who suffered from depression. He appeared to have it all: fine family, Ivy League education, very well respected in the community, very successful at what he did. But he was a bully and a cheater, and the truth was not one of his priorities. He had a life he kept secret from me, and he probably had some misogynistic tendencies.

"It was very painful for my kids to see me in a relationship with a man who was impatient, who was harsh, who would walk out of a room if it was not about him. I know he would have gotten better if he could have. I don't believe anyone wants to be selfish and angry. But he put me back in my childhood again. I lapsed into my people-pleasing mode of trying to make everything all right. Finally, I was able to look and see how much this man was like Jack.

"I was reliving Jack all over again, and I knew I had to come out the other side. But to achieve that was like being imprisoned in a large oil can and trying to climb out. My fingers were always slipping back, never able to get a grip. I was exhausted being in this relationship. I knew full well that I had worked hard and I deserved my success and happiness. But it was very difficult for me to extricate myself from that toxic relationship. Sometimes with him, I'd still feel Jack's ugly energy. Unfortunately those people don't leave your thoughts entirely. You must always fight them off.

"My childhood affects many aspects of my life in one way or another. I'm fifty-three, and in lots of ways I have a dreamy life. But there's always that little piece inside—that frightened little girl who ran into a dark room and locked the door."

"I Didn't Tell Anyone for Years"

Michelle, in her fifties now, has the dark hair and sexy figure she inherited from her mother. She has been married for twenty-five years to Peter, whom she describes as kind, comfortable to be with, understanding, and not demanding. They have two children.

Michelle spontaneously and almost immediately told me that when she met Peter, he was a great comfort to her, because she had a lot of social anxiety surrounding dating and what she referred to as "sexual etiquette." She was frequently ambivalent regarding sex: she sometimes felt that she wanted to have sex, but at the same time she felt uncomfortable, anxious, or even threatened when a man she dated made sexual advances. This would make her pull back, and when she did she, she would feel guilty because it seemed unfair for her to date someone without considering his needs as well as hers.

Michelle said that Peter was a "gem" because he managed to let her know that he wanted to be close and affectionate without ever seeming to make demands. She said, "It was like he sensed that I would be frightened if he was aggressive or tried to take control, so he kind of let me take the lead in determining what we did sexually." She found this attitude on his part to be "sexually liberating" for her. He was the first man with whom she ever had an orgasm.

Only after telling me about her husband did Michelle direct her attention to her father, whom she described as a "West Point graduate and a rigid disciplinarian, but also a good-looking man who was strong, intelligent, and had a great sense of humor." She described her parents as an "odd couple": her mother was a sexy Italian who was ten years younger than her father. They met while he was stationed in Europe. Michelle told me that after her father left the military and returned to the United States, he had a difficult time readjusting to civilian life, and he drank quite a lot.

"As a child, I didn't understand what the problem was. I just knew that sometimes there was this man who was very nice, and sometimes there was this man who was very scary. He would get violent. I can remember, he used to hit me, he used to hit my mother. There were scenes with the fists going through the door. My father was awful to my mother. I remember her having black eyes.

"My father was very competitive, even with his children. When we played games, he would get very angry if I won. He was also strict, and if I didn't do things the way he wanted, he would get physical, take out the strap, and make me go stand in a corner. But he could also be a lot of fun. When we were driving in the car, we'd sing songs and play word games.

"He taught me how to ride a bike, how to swim. His method was to throw you in the water. 'Now you better swim, because if you don't swim, you'll drown.'

"When I was six, my parents got divorced. At first, after the divorce, he continued to see my sister and me. We'd go on holidays with his family—my grandfather, who owned a pub in Massachusetts and had sparkling blue eyes and always wore a straw hat and carried a cane, and my grandmother, a lovely woman who used to take me to play bingo with the ladies at church.

"Sometimes my father would come to see us on weekends. He still loved my mother very much, and he didn't want her to divorce him. He kept trying to reestablish a relationship with her, and he assumed she wouldn't be able to survive without him. He kept coming to the house because he thought she would have to get back with him. He thought of her as a weak woman who would never be able to make it on her own.

"But she went to secretarial school and became a very good secretary. Then she became an airline stewardess. She did what she had to do to survive. The way that she was going to make her life was through men—relationships she had with men."

Michelle did not say so explicitly, but I had the impression from this remark that her mom took money from men. I don't know if she would fall into the category of a high-class prostitute or simply a very attractive woman who was not averse to accepting gifts from a sugar daddy. But certainly "did what she had to do to survive" implies some behavior that Michelle regarded as morally questionable.

"When I was eleven and my sister was nine, my father finally realized that there was no chance she'd take him back. So at that point, he absconded. He moved from state to state to avoid having to pay child support. My sister and I never heard from him again."

When Michelle's mother began working as an airline stewardess, the frequent periods away from home made her decide to put her two daughters in a foster home. The woman who took them in, along with four other children, was not horrible, not physically cruel, but she made no attempt to mother the children in her care. Her foster mother simply made sure their physical needs were taken care of. Rules were strictly enforced: eat all the food on your plate or sit there until you do; if you need to use the bathroom during the night, go down from the second floor to the basement and use the one down there. These strictures did nothing to make the girls feel at home, but they were not unbearable. However, their foster father made that time a nightmare.

"He would come out into the hallway by my room," says Michelle, "and he would be stark naked. He would stand there and look to see if I was awake. Then he would come into my room, and he would turn me over so I was on my stomach. He was just totally into my butt. I'd freeze. He'd stroke his penis, then rub it against my ass. It was so gross. When I'd wake up and see him standing there, I'd try to hide under my covers.

"To this day I can't have anybody do anything to my ass. I'm totally freaked out about that. Still, to this day. He had these worker's hands, with calluses on them, and I'd feel like—yuck—horrible. I didn't tell anyone for years. I was really, really worried that he was going to do the same thing to my little sister, but he never did."

As Michelle was telling me about the abuse she experienced at the hands of her foster father, she hesitated for a minute and then she blurted out, "My father was also slightly weird sexually."

When I asked what she meant, she retreated. "I mean, he would—he was slightly abusive . . . I don't want to go into it."

"Abusive with both you and your sister, or only you?"

"Me," she replied, reaching for her purse and beginning to fiddle with the strap as though at any minute she might bolt.

"Sexually abusive?"

"Yes."

"Did your mother know?"

"No. Nobody, nobody knows. Except my husband. I only told him after we'd been married for twenty-five years. Finally I could talk about it. It was like the genie in the bottle. In fact, I wasn't even sure it really happened, I had kept it so repressed."

"Did it just happen once?" I asked. "Or was it often?"

"Multiple times. And it was really awful since later on when I was put in a foster home, the same thing happened again with the man in that house."

Finally able to talk, Michelle was unsure what to say next. Then she continued.

"I used to get really angry with my husband, just go ballistic, and he would wonder where it was from. But it was all of these things that I had kept bottled up for a really long time. Once in a while my husband would do something that would really, really offend me in some way, really deeply offend me, and I would go ballistic. This horrible rage would come out. I think it was a real anger at men, you know, like, 'How dare you!' I realized later that it wasn't just anger with my husband. It was this anger that I'd never really dealt with."

The sexual abuse, Michelle said, occurred on weekend visits to her father after her parents were divorced when she was six and continued until her father disappeared when she was eleven.

"My sister doesn't know, and that's one of the reasons that I won't go with her to see my father now. What am I going to revisit? There's nothing to say to him after all these years. When I was sixteen, I got in touch with him to tell him that I'd gotten a scholarship to a very good prep school. Then later I called again when I was given a scholarship to college. I was excited, and I thought he'd be excited too. Instead he said to me, 'Why don't you just make money the way your mother did, on your back?'

"He never tried to contact me, but I did let him know when I graduated from college, and I did let him know when I married and moved to England. By then he lived in Connecticut, married to a widow who had inherited a lot of money. I remember when I got pregnant. I thought, 'Oh, I hope I have a son.' And I wanted to have sons, because I wanted to have some really good relationships with men. I just thought this could be so nice. I'm going to see what it's like to see a little boy growing up. And as it turned out, both of my children were boys. I wrote to my father, because I thought maybe knowing that he had grandsons would make him get in touch. But he never did. Ever.

"When I was growing up, I always wanted to please," says Michelle, her face breaking into the warm smile that draws people to her. "I would try so hard to get along with everyone at school and to be liked, because I needed so much to feel like somewhere there was something worthwhile about me—that people would like me or my teachers would like me. And do you know what happened?" Now she begins to laugh. "At school, my friends gave me the nickname 'Saccharine'—like you're just trying to be so sweet all the time. I had to deal with that, too. What do you do?"

The impact of the sexual abuse that Michelle experienced at the hands of her father and her foster father is clear from her story. She entered her young adulthood with real ambivalence regarding sex, and she was indeed fortunate that she met a man who seemed to sense this and make it clear to her that she could initiate and orchestrate their lovemaking. Michelle still experiences some sexual inhibitions, although she and Peter seem to be able to work around these pretty well.

The Path to Recovery

When children are abused by their fathers or stepfathers, they often experience not only acute distress at the time of the abuse, but also residual psychosocial adjustment difficulties that may persist well into adulthood or even last a lifetime.

Women who have been verbally, physically, or sexually abused by an angry father often suffer from posttraumatic stress disorder (PTSD). These women may manifest an extreme startle effect when they see or hear someone get angry, even if the anger is not directed toward them. They may be generally anxious and fearful, and they may have difficulty interacting socially, even on a casual level. They may have particular difficulty forming close, trusting relationships. They have also been found to be more likely than other adult women to suffer from eating disorders, substance abuse, compulsive spending or gambling, and other forms of self-destructive behavior.

Women who have experienced some form of sexual abuse are also likely to have various forms of sexual dysfunction as adults. They may be ambivalent about sex. They may act out sexually, engaging in compulsive or promiscuous sexual activity. They may enter the sex trade industry.

Many adult women experience these problems as adults without ever realizing the source of the difficulty. This is partly because abuse exists along a continuum, and it can be difficult to recognize when questionable behavior crosses the line to become truly abusive. Was your father simply a bit sarcastic when he criticized you, or did he insult and mock you to the point of verbal assault? Was he simply an "old school" dad who didn't hesitate to smack you to get your attention when you were misbehaving, or did he physically assault you in order to vent his own anger or cause you pain? Was he simply a "touchy-feely" guy, or was he sexually assaulting you for his own sexual gratification?

Sometimes women don't realize that their difficulties are related to abuse experienced in childhood because they defensively block out their memories of the abuse. An abused child may dissociate from the abusive experience at the time so as to avoid experiencing it. Margaret was engaging in a form of dissociation when she "shut out the insults" by closing her eyes.

But the daughters of abusive fathers can recover from the symptoms of PTSD, feelings of low self-worth, and problems with sexual dysfunction. Often this occurs spontaneously with the benefit of time and the experience of relationships with trustworthy partners. Sometimes recovery is facilitated by participation in reparative experiences, such as peer support groups for women who have histories of abuse. I will have more to say about such experiences in Part Two of this book.

Chapter Five

~ ❧ ~

The Unreliable Father

All of the fathers I have considered to this point had psychological problems that have actual diagnostic labels. In the chapter on disapproving fathers, I described men who have an attachment disorder. These men were unable to love and validate their daughters, because they lacked the capacity to form any deep emotional bond, even a bond to a child who is their own flesh and blood.

In the chapter on mentally ill fathers, I considered a man with schizophrenia, a man with obsessive-compulsive personality disorder, and two men who had bipolar personality disorder (manic-depression). These are all traditional psychiatric diagnoses.

In the chapter on substance-abusing fathers, I considered two alcoholics and a third father who abused both alcohol and a variety of other drugs. Substance addiction of many different types is identified and described in terms of a variety of criteria in a series of diagnostic labels in the American Psychiatric Association's *Diagnostic and Statistical Manual of Mental Disorders* corresponding to various forms of addiction.

Finally, in the chapter on abusive fathers, I described men who were verbally abusive, physically abusive, and sexually abusive. These behaviors are all related to psychological problems, including anger management and impulse control, and they too have specific diagnostic labels.

In this chapter, we consider a somewhat different group of fathers. These men are not connected by a common psychiatric diagnosis or set of diagnoses. They did not have a problem loving their children and did not perpetrate any acts of verbal, physical, or sexual abuse. They were simply unreliable. They may have been irresponsible, or preoccupied, or incompetent. But in any case, they were unreliable. They could not be depended on to perform basic parenting duties, show up on time, keep their promises, or provide economic security for their families.

Daughters of such fathers typically respond in one of two ways to the uncertainty generated by their undependable fathers. Some of these daughters assume that they must have done something wrong to cause their fathers to behave in this manner, and they tend to redouble their efforts to please. Others assume that all men are like their fathers: not to be believed, trusted, or relied on. Either assumption is a prescription for potential difficulties in future relationships.

Although the failures of these unreliable fathers may not be the direct result of any specific identifiable psychiatric disorder, their unreliability is likely to affect their daughters' attitudes toward men. Negative attitudes toward men formed during childhood and adolescence may alter the course of a daughter's life, and such attitudes can potentially represent significant obstacles to the daughters' adult psychosocial adjustment and life satisfaction.

"He Never Really Knew What Being a Father Was All About"

Lena is an attractive thirty-seven-year-old special education teacher. She has a fresh, healthy, "country" quality about her and exudes a sense of happiness and contentment. She lives in Winnipeg, Manitoba. Lena is a lesbian, and she lives with her partner of eleven years, Karen. Karen is an art teacher who works in the same school district as Lena.

When I asked Lena to tell me about her father, she described him as "warm, loving, and fun loving—*mostly* fun loving.

"We grew up in Cranbrook, British Columbia, probably one of the most beautiful places in the world. When I was very small, my dad was a physical education teacher and the hockey coach at the high school there, but he had this job for only five or six years.

When I was about eleven, he and some friends took over a minor league hockey franchise in Grande Prairie, Alberta, and throughout my high school years, he ran back and forth between B.C. and Alberta trying to make a go of this team. My mom was an elementary special education teacher. It's a good thing she was, too, because it was her steady income that supported my brother and me throughout our adolescence.

"Mom and Dad (Beth and Rory) were high school sweethearts. They have lived their whole lives in Cranbrook, except for the time they spent in college in Calgary. They were so much in love. They still are. Dad was the school hockey star, and he went to university in Calgary on a full athletic scholarship. He is pretty intelligent, but he was never much of a student. He just never studied. But he got through high school with pretty good grades, partly because the curriculum was not challenging and partly because his status as the school hockey star led all of the teachers to go easy on him and give him every break imaginable.

"One time he and Mom were talking about school, and she said something like, 'You never had to turn in your papers on time.'

"Dad replied that she was right, except that 'most of the time I never had to turn in my papers at all.' "

Lena said that her mom and dad had gone to the same college, and they started living together during their sophomore year.

"Mom and Dad had a great college experience. They loved each other. Dad loved hockey and enjoyed his physical education courses, which were clearly made easy for the athletes. Mom loved her special education courses. School was easy for her as well, and she gave Dad a lot of help with the few papers that he had to do for required courses that were out of his department. They had many friends. Everyone on the hockey team and nearly everyone involved in physical education loved both of them. They spent summers hiking and camping in the Canadian Rockies. They were both health nuts. They still are.

"Because of his star status on the hockey team, Dad was given a lot of free trips and a lot of free stuff in exchange for endorsements and things like hanging out at auto dealerships on Saturdays. He played some junior hockey as well as playing for the college team, and he might have been drafted by an NHL team, except that he had a couple of knee injuries that made his durability as a professional questionable. But no matter—they were really happy in school, and they had no trouble landing jobs back home in the same school district in which they had grown up.

"Mom got pregnant with me in their senior year, and they were married here in Cranbrook shortly after graduation. I was born that summer. They moved back to Cranbrook right after school. With some help from each of their two families, they bought a little house. Two years later, my little brother was born.

"I remember my dad as very affectionate toward me and my brother. He was very physical, and he hugged us, and wrestled with us, and tickled us. Once in a while, he and Mom would take us on hikes. But I also remember that a lot of the time, Dad wasn't around, and we spent a lot of time with Mom and her friends.

"Dad never really understood what being a father was all about. He was always preoccupied with other stuff. He liked coaching hockey a lot, and he was very friendly with his players. They were more like his friends or his younger brothers than like his students. They would hang out together a lot doing guy things like playing football and watching sports. They went to sports bars to watch big games, and whole groups of them would take off days at a time to go fishing and hunting. Over several summers Dad ran a fishing guide service, and the guides he hired were his current and former students. I remember distinctly feeling jealous of those young men. They had him, and I didn't.

"I remember one time—I must have been about seven or eight—he brought a bunch of his former students over to the house to watch the Grey Cup football championship game. They were all cheering and yelling and screaming. Then someone got mad and said the wrong thing, and suddenly there was a big brawl that lasted maybe five minutes. I mean, there were these big guys all wrestling around on the floor and taking swings at each other, and my dad was right there in the middle of it. Then it stopped as quick as it started, and everyone shook hands and hugged each other and went back to watching the game.

"No hard feelings—literally. But the whole thing kind of freaked me out. I remember thinking to myself, 'My God, these men are like wild animals. You never know when they will be around, and when they're around you never know when there's going to be a brawl.'

"It was shortly after that when my dad bought into the hockey team in Grande Prairie. I remember Mom and Dad had one of the few fights I can ever remember them having, because Dad took all their savings and took out a loan to buy his share. Mom didn't like that at all, and she didn't like the fact that Dad had decided to quit teaching to become the general manager of a minor league hockey team located way up in northern Alberta. But in the end, Mom accepted his decision. She loved him, and she knew who he was.

"After that, things were a little rough. First of all, we went from being very comfortable financially to just about getting by. We lived on Mom's salary, because Dad couldn't ever make that hockey franchise produce enough income to draw a salary. But he loved it. He loved hanging out with the players, and he loved trying to promote ticket sales and sell advertising. He loved it when someone from a newspaper would interview him, even if the newspaper was only the local *Grande Prairie Examiner*.

"In addition, Dad was away more than he was home. He was gone for weeks at a time, then home a few days, then gone again. Grande Prairie is a long way from Cranbrook, and Dad wasn't commuting in a private jet. He drove back and forth. It was like twelve hours. Sometimes when the weather was bad, he would get stuck up there when he was supposed to be home. Often he would promise to be with us for some family function and then not make it. I remember he missed one Christmas entirely when his team got in some playoff. From time to time we all complained and asked him to come back to Cranbrook and go back to teaching at the high school. He could have done it any time.

"But he wasn't about to come back. He liked what he was doing. He liked his freedom. He liked his little apartment between the hockey rink and the feed store in Grande Prairie. He liked hanging out with his players and partying. I have a feeling he may have had a few extramarital flings as well—not affairs as much as one-night stands that came from hanging out with the players in sports bars and strip joints.

"My mom alternated between bitching and begging him to come back home to live, but all to no avail. And through it all, there was never a hint that she might leave him or ask for a divorce. She loved him a lot, and basically she was willing to do whatever she had to do to have him for as much of the time as she could have him, even if it was bloody little time.

"I was probably more angry at my father than my mom was—or at least I showed it more. I was angry because he wasn't there for me. He missed events that were important to me. I played soccer all through school, but he wasn't interested in girls' sports. So even if he was home, he wouldn't bother coming. He'd rather hang with his students and former students. I remember thinking, he loves them because they idolize him, but I idolize him too, and that doesn't seem to matter. I got a lot more attention and praise from Mom and her female friends.

"I was also mad at Dad because he really hurt Mom. She was lonely a lot. But she was also strong and resilient. She kept the house together and kept us fed. She came to my soccer games when she could, and she was always there to talk to me. Like a rock.

"Sometimes I think the strength I saw in my mom and the real positive feedback I got from her friends explains, at least partly, why I ended up feeling more comfortable with women than with men. Certainly I have a much deeper and more trusting relationship with my partner, Karen, than I can ever imagine having with a man. It's not that I find the thought of having sex with a man repulsive. I've been there and done that. But when you talk about a solid, permanent, committed relationship, I can only think of Karen.

"I never came home to tell Mom, 'I'm gay.' I came home to tell her that I was in love with Karen and we were going to be together.

She was wonderful. She not only said that she understood. She was empathic. She told me that there were many times when she felt that she felt closer emotionally to some of her female friends than she did to Dad.

"But then she smiled wistfully and said, 'But I sure do love him.'

"That's another reason why I was so angry at my dad for being so selfish and immature with his life. Here he had this woman who adored him, and whom he adored, but he never grew up and recognized that she needed him full time. He never realized that he had a family who wanted him to be with them a lot, not always off coaching hockey or fishing with a bunch of younger guys who didn't have his responsibilities.

"I have never confronted Dad in anger, though I have made sarcastic remarks to the effect that he never really knew us because he was never around. To his credit, he was fine with me when I told him about Karen. But his attitude was more like, 'If that's what you want, go for it.' He never asked what it was about Karen that attracted me to her. He never asked me when it was that I realized that I didn't want a man for a partner. And he certainly never asked why.

"Eventually Dad sold his interest in the hockey franchise and came back to Cranbrook, where he coaches junior hockey. Mom is happier because she sees him more now, and she still loves him to death. Dad is happier too, mainly because he realizes on some level that he was just getting too old to be riding around Canada in a bus shepherding his players to and from their away games. And I'm happy as well. I'm happy that they have each other, and I'm happy that I have Karen."

Lena's response to her father's irresponsibility and lack of dependability seems to have been to conclude that men are not to be relied on. They are too selfish and never really grow up. They are not there when you need someone to confide in. They may not even be capable of understanding the types of concerns you might want to share. In contrast, women like her mother, some of her mother's friends, and her partner are reliable, mature, and understanding.

"A Man Can't Have Two Families and Be There for Either One"

Virginia is a fifty-two-year-old poet who teaches English at a university in the Midwest. Even now, in middle age, she finds it difficult to talk about her childhood. A woman awash in words, she slipped into the third person when she began to talk about the way she felt about her father.

"I've just opened the door on this little girl, who has been hidden away from me for all these years. I think that she's probably about age five, and she's falling apart. She was probably madly in love with her daddy—a nice little sunny girl who liked to dress up and please her daddy. She just wanted to believe in him."

Suddenly the little girl who came out of hiding after all these years stepped aside, and Virginia continued in the first person.

"By the time I was about five, my father was halfway out the door. He had been having an affair off and on with a woman in France since before he even met my mom. This affair continued throughout my childhood and adolescence. It ebbed and flowed, but I always had the feeling that the woman in France was his priority, and that he would leave us in a heartbeat if she asked him to be with her. Eventually she did, and he left. This happened when I was fourteen. They later married.

"The whole time my father had an apartment in Paris, and he made frequent trips there. The trips were ostensibly connected with his business, but there was never any doubt that there was another woman there as well. Even as children, my sister and I could pick up on what was going on. My mother knew what was going on as well, but she put up with it, hoping it would go away. I believe that she was under the impression that the other woman was also married or otherwise unavailable, and that in the end, the affair would peter out, and her marriage to my father would survive.

"However, as time went on, she began to realize that my father's lover was his priority and that the affair was not about to fade away. She also realized that he would leave her for this other woman if she became available. As this recognition sunk in, my mother got more and more depressed. There were fights in the kitchen. So, as I said, from pretty early, on I must have known he had one foot out the door. A child doesn't know how to deal with that.

"My mother got more and more depressed, but nobody talked about what was going on. But just before my dad left, my mom began working full time. She must have realized on some level that she had better prepare for the inevitable. She became an editor at a literary magazine. This was pretty heavy-duty work, with substantial demands on her time. So pretty soon my father was gone completely and my mother was out of the house most of the time working. So we really lost both parents. I did see my father occasionally after he and Mom were divorced, but these occasions were irregular and infrequent.

"The only person we had around us on a dependable basis was Mary, who was our nanny. But she was more a support for my sister, because Mary was very religious and my sister would go up to her room and read the Bible with her. Mary was wonderful and a Christian and a good woman, but she wasn't someone I could sit down with and talk about my feelings."

I asked Virginia directly how she would describe the impact of her father's having his foot out the door throughout her childhood. She said that she could not really explain the dynamics, but she was convinced that his undependability had affected her relationships with men.

"Before I met and married my husband, I lived with a very crazy poet who'd been a protégé of the famous poet W. H. Auden. I had been experiencing some symptoms of anxiety that I thought were related to my parents. And the poet came along right around this time, and one of the things he said was, 'You've got to get away from thinking about your parents. You have to just evolve into your own life.'

"Somehow at the time I thought that these words were very profound, and I moved in with him. I stayed with him for a few years. He had a huge IQ, but he was also really crazy. He was intense and emotional, and sometimes I would say something that would set him off, and he'd attack me physically. And whenever that happened, I would blame myself. That screwed-up relationship lasted for about two years.

"In the midst of this, I was hired by the university, and that's where I met Bill, the man who would become my husband. I started having lunch with Bill, and he was like a white knight. I won't say he dragged me out of that bad relationship. But it just happened. By then I had actually moved out of the poet's apartment, but he wasn't completely out of the picture yet. It took Bill to save me from that abuse. It makes me think of Dante—I'd been brought out from hell into the light.

"When I first brought Bill home, my mother said, 'There's nothing negative about him, but there's nothing very positive about him either.' She couldn't see his depth.

"The irony is I found somebody who worked well with me and, given my background, that's unusual. I mean, I suppose it's a miracle that I didn't go after someone like my father.

"Still, it took ten years of living together with Bill before we got married, so there was probably a part of me that thought Bill should be more flamboyant or more charming or speak up more. But the reality was that I was happy with him. And I am happy with him still. Best of all, he's a terrific father."

Virginia grew up with no one on whom she could depend for emotional support. Her father was constantly threatening to disappear even during her earliest recollections, and ultimately he did pretty much disappear. Her mother was chronically depressed and lacked the capacity for emotional closeness.

It's not surprising that Virginia's first serious sexual relationship was with a brilliant but crazy poet. At least he was emotionally available, even if he was hot-tempered and abusive. Perhaps Virginia used the poet to experience the emotional involvement she had never felt from her parents. Only then was she ready to seek out and marry her dependable husband. With Bill, she has been able to obtain the security she was never able to obtain through her father.

"He Was a Wimp; He Had No Mass"

Sally, an attractive blonde woman in her fifties, is divorced with no children. She is the president of a large manufacturing company that produces fashionable clothing for children—the kind of extravagant outfits that doting grandmothers buy. Although she is clearly a successful executive with a take-charge attitude, she is modest. In fact, she gives herself so little credit for her accomplishments that it seems as if her perceptions are out of touch with reality.

"People tell me not to say this, but I can't help it. I say it all the time: I think the reason I became successful was that I was in the right place at the right time."

To appreciate how self-effacing this assessment is, consider that Sally has spent years building a successful company in a highly competitive industry. She has consistently displayed both creative talent and managerial skill. She has an instinctive sense of how to put colors and fabric together so that they catch the eye, and she is famous for inspiring loyalty in both her staff and her customers. In addition to her accomplishments in business, she has contributed a great deal to the community. She established and runs a foundation to help babies born with AIDS that has raised a great deal of money for research and established treatment centers in five urban locations.

Because I knew full well both her business and charitable accomplishments, I challenged Sally's observation that she had simply been in the right place and the right time. I wasn't too diplomatic in my follow-up to her description. I said, "You can't be serious."

When pushed in this manner, Sally stopped speaking for some time and closed her eyes as if she was trying to solve a problem. I wasn't sure if I had offended her, or if she was wondering whether her self-perception was as far off base as I seemed to be suggesting. Finally she opened her eyes, looked at me, and said, "You know, you're right. It wasn't all luck. You're not the first person who has told me that luck had nothing to do with my working my way up in this industry and becoming the president of this company. I have worked very hard. From the day I started working, I felt an insatiable appetite to do better than anybody else. While others were going out and having drinks and a good time, I was trying to figure out how to do more work to get ahead—to prove that if they promoted me to a better job, I could do it."

But there is another reason for her success, and she finds that harder to accept. She has always been "Little Miss Fix-It," the person who smoothes out the trouble spots, reassures the insecure, and wants everyone to be happy.

"My first job was with a company that was falling apart—we were going to be sold to a new company, and people were frightened about what might happen to them. I reassured them that everybody was going to have jobs. Everything would be okay. Just keep your nose to the grindstone. I was the leader and inspiration in that office. These were men in their forties, and they had families to support. I was just twenty-one, fresh out of college. And I was the one who held the place together and gave strength to everyone. I think that my strength and my willingness to work hard got recognized."

I suggested to Sally that it seemed particularly remarkable that someone as young as she was at that time would become the leader in an office where many of the employees were older and more experienced. She responded that it was really not surprising, because for as long as she could remember, her father had acted very much like those frightened middle-aged male employees in her company.

"The way I acted when I started working was very similar to the way I felt that I had to behave during my adolescence. My father was a really sweet person. He would never hurt a fly. And he was affectionate. But he was incompetent. He was an inept office worker. He must have held twenty different jobs before I graduated from high school. He never got a promotion, and he frequently got fired. My ex-husband, Carl, once described my father as 'a wimp. He had no mass.' And that is a pretty accurate characterization.

"Even when he was working, he didn't earn a lot of money. And sometimes when he would get fired, it would be a long time before he got another job. During those periods, things were really rough.

My mom always worked, but she had no education. She was a sales-woman in a local department store, and she did babysitting at night for extra money. So when Dad wasn't working, we clearly did not have enough money to live. There were times when we didn't know where our next dinner was coming from.

"And I spent my childhood trying to make my mom and dad feel good and feel safe. I helped out by working myself. I did babysitting as far back as I can remember. I even did yard work for neighbors, even though it was mainly little boys who did this type of work at that time. I gave the money I made to my mom. I also reassured her constantly that things were "going to be all right." I made sure that I did very well in school so I could get a scholarship to college, and in college I took mostly business and economics courses. I wanted to make absolutely certain that I was better prepared to compete in the world of work than my father had been.

"So when I came to work at that first job, I found myself in a situation that was really quite similar to what I was used to at home. Things were bad economically. People were inept and apparently not able to make things better. And everyone was apprehensive about the uncertain future. Obviously I fit right in. I reassured everyone and kept morale up. I tried to motivate everyone to do whatever they could to help the company, even if they didn't feel that they could do a lot. And once the company was bought out, things did get better, and I got a promotion because everyone at the old company recommended me.

"Later on I had some good ideas for products that helped to turn the company around, and I was rewarded with further promotions. Then a headhunter approached me with an offer to become president here. So I guess it was really a combination of hard work and good fortune. And I suppose in a funny way, I have my dad to thank for my being so driven to succeed. Lord knows I never felt that anyone else was going to take care of me. I was always the one doing the 'taking care of.' The good fortune came when I landed up in my first job in a situation exactly suited to someone who made a habit of taking care of people.

"But I need to say that there was a downside to all this good fortune. First of all, I missed out on a lot of adolescent activities, because I was spending a lot of time working and a lot of time reassuring everyone. In addition, I missed out on a lot of young adult activities because I was so driven to be successful. I did miss the going out with the coworkers for drinks after work. I didn't miss it at the time, but I realize now it would have been fun, and it would have made me a more well-rounded person. I didn't date much, and when I finally did get involved in a relationship, I chose a man who was so much the opposite of my father that things didn't work out.

"My ex-husband, Carl, is a strong person who can take care of himself. He is opinionated and forceful. He represented security and power to me—everything my father was not. But Carl is a taker and a user. In fact, I shouldn't have said 'when I chose a man.' I should have said, 'when I allowed myself to be chosen by a man.' Carl came along after I had become fairly successful, and I believe now that he was attracted in part to my earning potential and to his belief that with my position, I could enhance his own career, which was in fashion marketing."

Ironically, however, Carl's driven quality came with a certain lack of emotional connection. "We looked good together. We were a kind of a minor-league power couple. But I was never really close to Carl. I now believe that when I married Carl, we were convenient to each other rather than in love. In fact, I don't know that Carl ever told me that he loved me.

"Just one day he said, 'We should get married.' And at the time it seemed like a good idea to me. We never even discussed the possibility of having children. Our conversations were almost always about the fashion industry or about particular issues that arose in each of our professional endeavors. And those conversations were good and often mutually rewarding. But they were more like discussions between coworkers than like the deep emotional sharing I would now want to have with a real life partner.

"About six years ago, I became involved with a group of women professionals who had formed a sort of mutual help network. They had regular meetings and ran retreats with speakers who talked a lot about achieving business success as well as personal fulfillment. I made some real friends there, and we talked a lot about trade-offs between business life and personal life. I found that many of the members of the group had the idea that they had given up a great deal personally to get where they were professionally. Many complained that they somehow wound up with men who were not emotionally available. That's when I realized that I had done just that. That epiphany ultimately led me to ask Carl for a divorce. His response was pretty much what I expected, which was pretty much, 'Yes, maybe you're right. I understand.'

"Now I am doing a good deal to develop other aspects of my personality. I started my foundation, and I have been feeling a lot more involved with the world around me and with people. I have also been doing some socializing, and I have met some people with whom I can really share my feelings. Who knows? Maybe I'll find a soulmate one of these days."

The Path to Recovery

In the stories of these three women, we can see plainly the impact of an unreliable father. It can make a woman assume responsibilities for supporting the family at a time in life when she should be learning how to relate to peers. It can make her a hard-working, driven individual who is successful but may fail to give herself credit for her achievements.

Having an unreliable father is quite likely to leave a daughter with the belief that men are not to be trusted or relied on. It may make the daughter self-reliant, but it may preclude or delay the possibility of establishing an emotionally intimate, trusting relationship with a loving man. She may find such a relationship with another woman, as Lena did, or she may get involved with a man who is inappropriate.

Virginia first sought out a "crazy poet" who was imbalanced and abusive, because at least he represented an emotional presence. But after she freed herself from the abusive poet, it took her years to come to the realization that she should marry Bill, who is steady as a rock but lacks some of the polish and sophistication of her unreliable father. Sally married a man who was forceful and competent, but emotionally unavailable. She was nearly fifty years old before she realized that security is not the only factor to consider in making important life decisions. It is possible to achieve security and still have an emotionally close trusting relationship.

In one sense, the lesson to be learned from the women in this chapter is similar to the lessons of the earlier chapters: a woman with a father who failed her for whatever reason cannot run her adult life on the assumption that all men will treat her as their father did. This lesson is not typically grasped spontaneously. One form of emotionally corrective experience of another is typically required. This may come in the form of validation and recognition derived through friends or work. It may come in the form of a corrective experience such as a support group or a therapist. Or it may come as a result of the good fortune of meeting and becoming involved with someone who is different from the father who failed her.

Chapter Six

The Absent Father

In this chapter I consider one final group of fathers who tend to create problems for their daughters: fathers who are unavailable to fulfill the basic parenting roles because they are literally absent. These men include fathers who die when their daughters are children or adolescents, fathers who abandon their daughters or fail to maintain a relationship with their daughters following a divorce, and fathers in name only, who spend little or no time in the physical presence of their children. These fathers create problems because they do not provide their daughters with a realistic model of desirable male behavior. They leave it up to the daughters to imagine what they are like, and accordingly they leave it up to their daughters to figure out what a good man might be like.

Among daughters who remember a father being present for a time when they were very young, the resulting fantasy is based on their cloudy recollections of what he was like before he left. In most cases, these daughters remember only the best of times with their fathers, and their fantasies are highly idealized. Among daughters who never knew their fathers at all, the fantasy is largely the product of the imagination, informed by Hollywood movies and novels, with the imagined father idealized as perfect in every way. In either case, the daughters of absent fathers often spend their early adulthood trying to find a man who conforms to the fantasy.

"Chasing Daddy All These Years"

Antonia had a close and loving relationship with her father, but he died when she was ten. Over the course of her lifetime, she has been attracted to men who were superficially similar to her dad. However, these men, including her husband of twenty-five years, from whom she is now divorced, have most often been lacking in the more substantial attributes required for a mutually satisfying relationship, forcing her to take charge and invent whatever additional attributes were required to fulfill her fantasy relationship.

When I asked Antonia to describe her relationship with her father, she began by declaring, "I've probably been chasing Daddy all these years. He was my friend. He was my play pal. He gave me a lot of affection. He was my partner against my mother when she was mad at me or yelling at me. I remember he would go into another room and call me to come with him. Then we would both giggle together. He and my mother had a very good relationship, because, although she had a temper, he always used humor to get her out of her bad mood.

"I was ten when he died of cancer, and though my memories of him aren't vivid, they're all incredibly positive. I remember he was tall and handsome and had a great sense of humor. My mother tells how, the night before he died, she thought he'd slipped into a coma, and so she put her mouth next to his ear and asked, 'Jack? Do you know who I am?'

"And he opened his eyes and looked at my mother—whose name was Mary—and said, 'What would you have done if I'd said, "Oh, Caroline, didn't we have fun together?" You'd be wondering for the rest of your life who Caroline was.'

"I can only remember once when he got angry with me. I must have been very young, because my mother was giving me castor oil, and I spit it out all over her clothes. My father grabbed me and put me in my room, pointing his finger at me and saying, 'Don't you ever do that again.'

"He was more assertive than my mother. He took care of everything. He drove her places. He paid all the bills, and all the finances went through him. Everybody got their allowance from him. When he died, my mother didn't know how to do anything. Obviously she learned, but she adored my father and she never did remarry.

"When the doctors diagnosed his cancer, they told my mother he'd be dead in six or seven months. She decided not to tell my father. Instead, she told me, making it clear that we were to keep the news from my father. And for the six months that he lived, we never did tell him, although of course by the end, he certainly knew that he was not going to get better.

"I remember thinking, 'I can't tell him, so I'm going to pretend it's not happening.' Then at the very end, when he was really sick, my mother brought him home, because he didn't want to die in the hospital, and she sent me out to stay with my aunt on Long Island. I remember feeling very isolated there, not knowing what was happening. My aunt was very kind and tried to keep me busy and, you know, took me fishing and to the beach.

"But I remember feeling that back in the city, something horrible was going on. At the very last moment my mother brought me back to New York. I remember the night that he died—the people coming from the funeral home to take him out of the house. She thought I was asleep, but I was awake and I heard it all. I was so upset, but I didn't want to get up because I was scared by the whole thing. And I refused to go to the funeral.

"Everyone told my mother, 'Don't force her.' Even now, talking about it, I could cry.

"Although my mom didn't marry again, there was an uncle who was very much involved in my life who was a wonderful man. And my mother did have, I guess, a boyfriend. She wouldn't refer to him as such. She called him a friend. But as I remember, he was a lovely man, and he came by once a week and he always brought me toys and played a lot and talked with me. He had been a friend of my father and his wife had schizophrenia. Since he was married, even though his wife was in an institution, the relationship never went beyond friendship.

"I think my memory of my father—and the loss of him—influenced all my romantic relationships: my choice of boyfriends, my choice of a husband. The men I chose were all the same. Each time I picked my father, and I continue to be attracted to men like my father—except for the tragic flaw, the cancer.

"I always began by honing in on the physical, which is tall and skinny, then the sense of humor. When those two things were in place, I was putty in the hands of a man. Even today I can't feel attracted to somebody short. I can't like somebody heavy. For me to want to kiss somebody, he has to be tall and skinny and have a sense of humor. And unfortunately that's not necessarily enough for a good marriage or a relationship. I really, really have tried to like people who aren't that type, but if they don't resemble my father and have his sense of humor, it simply won't work.

"In addition, beyond my lack of discrimination in the initial attraction and involvement, I immediately began to mistrust any man to whom I felt attracted, because I was always afraid that he was going to abandon me the way my father abandoned me. Then I would become very needy and clingy. It was very disconcerting to the men I dated. Some men, when they learned about my father dying when I was young, understood my fears of abandonment, but most did not. The result was that my fear that I would be abandoned became self-fulfilling: a relationship would start up, I would get clingy, and he would run.

Antonia eventually married a man who did not run, and she stayed married for nearly twenty-five years. Charles conformed superficially to her fantasy father. He is tall, thin, charming, and has a great sense of humor. And when Antonia became needy and possessive, he went right along with it. In fact, he enjoyed being possessed, because he enjoyed being taken care of. Charles really didn't measure up in many important areas, but she stayed with him because she knew that he would not leave her.

Antonia observed that her Charles "never held a steady job" and contributed only minimally to household finances and to the work of raising their two children. However, "Because I had this wonderful fantasy of him as a carbon copy of my father, I filled in the gaps. I let myself become the breadwinner. I provided everything we had. I ran the household. I looked after the children and dealt with their teachers and activities. I might as well have been single. I was beset with fatigue a lot in those years. I was just exhausted from balancing all the plates. The only things I ever got from Charles were two kids and an amusing partner to take to dinner parties."

When Antonia was forty-eight, she was diagnosed with breast cancer and had to go through surgery and a six-month course of chemotherapy. During this period, Charles was pretty useless. He couldn't cope with not being taken care of, and he certainly wasn't up to the task of taking care of Antonia. That chore fell to her children, now young adults. They complained a lot about their father's lack of involvement, but they knew him well and really didn't expect anything different.

Antonia didn't expect much from Charles either, but the cancer scare made her stop and think about what she was getting out of her life, and it hit her hard that she was getting very little from Charles. On top of all that, she participated in a cancer support group in which the major topic of discussion was getting support from your family. Antonia emerged from her illness cancer free and Charles free as well. Shortly after she knew that she was going to be okay, she asked for a divorce.

Antonia said that before her illness, she had some friends who suggested that Charles was not adding anything to her life. She said that they would ask her, "Why didn't you get a divorce?" At that point in her life, Antonia would respond, "I really don't have time to divorce him," meaning that she was too busy taking care of everything to schedule an appointment with a lawyer. After her illness, the same friends asked her why she had finally decided to get a divorce.

She told me that at this point she would respond to her friends that "I didn't have time *not* to divorce him," meaning that her cancer had made her realize that life is short and that she wanted a meaningful, mutually satisfying relationship with a man before she died.

"Charles and I split when the children were already grown up. They still see my ex-husband all the time, and they love him. But he's always been more of a sibling to them than a father. He's like a big play pal, my third child. He doesn't know how to be an adult."

Antonia hasn't yet found the mutually satisfying relationship that she is seeking, but she has great hope for the future. She admits that she is still attracted to tall, thin men with a sense of humor, but now she knows enough not to restrict her dating to men who fit these superficial characteristics. She observed humorously, "When you are nearly fifty and you are looking for a man, you can't afford to limit the field anyway. I am almost forced to take a second look at any man who comes calling, even if he doesn't look like Dad."

"He Still Feeds Me"

Looking back, Anne can remember a happy time before her father left: "I'd wake up really early in the morning and go into my parents' bedroom and climb into bed with them. They'd sing, 'Oh what a beautiful morning . . .'"

Her father was handsome and strong and loving. She remembers him making breakfast for her and her mother. She remembers that he was a very good cook, because he had worked as a chef before he opened the restaurant that he ran during those early years. She has pictures of herself as a toddler riding on her father's shoulders. In the pictures, her fingers are clutching his hair, and their smiles make it quite clear that they were both truly happy.

But then it all ended. Anne is still not clear what happened, but she remembers her parents arguing and her mother crying and throwing things at her father. She remembers him hugging her and telling her, "I have to leave for a while. I love you." And she never saw him again.

Anne knows there was a bitter divorce and a battle over custody and visitation. She knows that her mother hates her father to this day. She doesn't know why. Her mother wouldn't ever tell her what caused the breakup of the marriage. Her mother would only tell her, "The best thing I ever did was getting that bastard out of our lives."

Anne later learned from her mother's sister that her mother had made it pretty much impossible for her father to see Anne after he walked out that night, and after a while he gave up trying. Then he moved away to parts unknown. Anne doesn't know whether he left to protect her from the spectacle of seeing her mother and father fight, or whether he couldn't stand the fighting himself, or whether he got worn down with all the fighting, or whether he simply didn't give a damn. She only knows that he gave up and left.

In the absence of any clues about what might have happened, Anne chose to believe that he had left to protect her. Anne told me that her mother was indeed a difficult person. She was demanding, and she had a bad temper. She was occasionally prone to drink too much wine. As Anne grew up, they fought a good deal. Most of the battles were manifestations of typical adolescent strivings for separation, but from Anne's descriptions, it does sound as if their conflicts had a bit more of an edge than normal. At any rate, Anne's view of her mother was sufficiently negative as to allow her to imagine that her father was a loving and considerate man who had left to save his daughter from witnessing conflicts between her mother and father.

Anne built on her early memories of the good times with her father to construct an idealized fantasy father. Then she proceeded to run her life in a manner that she thought might please this fantasy father. She was an English major in college, and when she finished school, she got a job as the food editor of a regional tourist magazine. Later she became a food and wine critic for a national magazine that focused on four-star inns and fine dining.

In her early adult years, "I was attracted to many of the restaurant owners and chefs I met during the course of writing articles. I was easily seduced by a man who wanted to feed me and knew how to do it well. I generally got very good treatment from the restaurant owners and chefs I met, because they were all quite aware that my reporting could make or break their businesses. So right from the start, almost every new review that I wrote offered some potential for a romantic outcome, and I took advantage of many of these encounters. I'm not saying I never dated a lawyer or an actor, but I met more chefs than anyone else, and it was only natural that I would go out with them."

But Anne did not run off the deep end and marry the first good-looking chef whose restaurant she reviewed. She frequently had brief flings and even one-night trysts with some of the men she met this way, but she did not mistake the attraction associated with their professional need to feed her with more enduring qualifications for building a satisfying a long-term relationship.

Perhaps because her father had abandoned her so early and she had so few detailed memories of who he was, her fantasy template of her father was incomplete. As a result, Anne was left free to choose among the men she dated on the basis of other characteristics that were not derived from her father's image.

"I guess it was pretty much predetermined that I would end up marrying a chef or a restaurant owner, but beyond that, I was on my own, so to speak. And I dated like this for five or six years before I met someone I felt I wanted more from than a good meal, good wine, and good sex. When I met John, however, I started thinking beyond these gratifications very quickly.

"John was the owner and executive chef of a trendy nouvelle cuisine restaurant in the Berkshires [in Massachusetts]. When I met John, I found him very attractive. He was warm and happy and cuddly, and he enjoyed life. He was a bit older than me, and he was divorced. He had two children, and he was the custodial parent. Their mother had drug problems and was in and out of rehab all the time, so John took over. Well, I guess I don't have to draw you a picture. John had all the good qualities that I knew my father had, and he also had what my father never had: his children.

"You can't imagine how much I relished John's affection. Almost from the moment I met him, I saw him taking care of me: feeding me, giving me material to write about in the magazine, sheltering me before the fireplace in his restaurant, and allowing me to participate in his life with his children. I was hooked from the start.

"When we started dating, I planned from the start to win him over and make him my husband. He was more cautious, perhaps just because he was older and wiser, but perhaps also because he was a little gun shy from his first marriage and cautious about how his children would respond to a new woman who was more than just a casual friend or a date.

"It took some time to work through some of these issues, but before too long, we transitioned into a family. This added a whole new level of satisfaction to the relationship for me, because I found myself reliving those early years that I had when my parents were still together.

"So John and I got married, and we are living happily ever after. We have his two kids, and two we had together. Of course, we have had some of the ups and downs that stepfamilies have. John is a bit of a perfectionist, and he's tougher with the kids than I would be. But then he's a chef, so he must be a perfectionist. And I always felt that with his kids, I had to back off. He is still warm and jolly. He still feeds me. He feeds us all."

So Anne weathered the storm of losing her father and emerged happy and intact. She constructed a fantasy of the father who left her, and she found men who seemed to match this fantasy. Unlike Antonia, she didn't latch on to the first man and every other man who matched the most basic attributes of the fantasy father. Rather she used the fantasy as an initial screening device, and then she took a closer look at other characteristics of the potential partner.

In John she found attributes of a more complete partner than the original fantasy. John could have had horrible negative qualities that might have doomed the relationship in the long term, but fortunately he does not seem to have any such skeletons in the closest. He is not perfect, but he is very good. Anne has a very good understanding of how she got to be where she is, and she is happy to be there.

"I Never Knew My Father Because He Was Never at Home"

Delphine is a thirty-four-year-old FBI agent, married to a Drug Enforcement Administration (DEA) agent. She told me that she is very happily married. They have no children, Delphine explained, because both she and her husband are "married to their jobs as well as to each other, and there is just no room for children."

Delphine offered spontaneously that she is quite sure that her career choice is related to her image of her father, now deceased, who was an officer in the U.S. Army Special Forces for fourteen years before he was killed in action in the Philippines. She said that she never knew her father because he was never at home.

"When I say never, I mean almost literally never. He had been in the service for six years before I was born, and during the eight years that he was alive after I was born, I remember seeing him only twice. One time I think I was about four, and the other time I think I was maybe seven. I know him mostly from pictures my mother had—mostly pictures of him in uniform in a formal pose. And I know him as well from the stories I hear from my older brother and sister, and my dad's friend Samuel, who first shared my mother's grief over my dad's death and later became my mother's significant other.

"I have one memory of me sitting on his lap and him tickling me and swinging me around over his head. That was when I was four, and there is a picture of me with him taken that day. I remember that I was thrilled to see him and be with him. I also remember that I got a lot of attention that day because my brother and sister stayed away from him. They knew him better, and they were a little afraid of him. Apparently he was rather gruff and intimidating. But I don't really know about that. I just remember being thrilled that day when he was playing with me.

"The other memory I have is from about three years later. I remember him returning home from a tour of duty in the Mideast. I remember him coming through a gate at an airport somewhere, and I remember him hugging my mother for a long, long time. I waited for him to hug me too, and he did, but only for a second. He was interested only in my mom. They came home with us kids, but then they left right away for R&R somewhere by themselves. They left us with my dad's parents, who were visiting from New York just so they could babysit and give mom and dad a chance to be away and alone together.

"The funny thing is that I don't remember anything else from that time he was home, even though I have been told that he was home for several months. I don't think he was around the house at all then. I don't know what he was doing, but it wasn't with us. And then he was off again on duty, and that's when he was killed.

"I remember when they told my mom he had died. She was a basket case for weeks. I mean, one thing is for sure: she really loved him. But it must have been a strange life, being in love with someone who was around for only a few months every couple of years. I know she was lonely, and I know she had a few affairs while he was gone. But she loved him, and she glorified him so. You can't believe what she would say about how patriotic and dedicated he was to his country. I must have heard the words *duty* and *sacrifice* a million times when I was a kid.

"But I also remember as a kid that I was jealous of my friends whose fathers were present in their lives. I remember one time, just before my father was killed, talking to a friend who was complaining that her dad wouldn't let her watch a certain television program. I remember thinking that I would be willing to take the chance of missing a TV program or two if I could have my dad close to me so I could sit on his lap again—and then of course he was killed.

"But his figure remained a strong factor in my life, even after he died. My mom never forgot him, and she never failed to say something nice about him on special days like his birthday, their anniversary, and the date he was killed. Even after she started dating other men, even after she began living with his friend, he was never forgotten. I remember one time my mom and her boyfriend, Samuel, stood together in the living room of our house and drank a toast to my dad's memory—and then went off to the bedroom to make love.

"My mom was kind of black and white in her views on things. There were army people, who were the salt of the earth and larger than life, and then there were the rest of the people in the country, whom she saw basically as weak, indolent cowards who didn't have enough sense to know what the army people were doing to save their miserable asses.

"So it's not surprising that I went to college on an army ROTC scholarship and became a lieutenant in the army. What's surprising is that I didn't stay in for life. But I didn't like the army. It was too restrictive for me, and I was always afraid that I would be sent off to some horrible place to work, and maybe even get killed like my dad. I wanted to have a regular home and to know that I could live in that home full time.

"So I got out at the end of my obligation and joined the FBI. That was easy, because I had been in the military police in the service. I think being an MP is another reason why I didn't stay in the service. When you're an MP, you really see the uglier side of military life: the drunks and the brawls and the spousal abuse. I couldn't deal with any of that, at least not for an entire career.

"So the FBI kind of gave me an out. I could still serve my country, which kept me from entering the ranks of the indolent civilians who were being protected by the army people, but it let me have a life. In fact, it gave me a nice clean office job and a home in the suburbs.

"Meanwhile, since I've been old enough to be interested in men, I've been attracted to strong men in uniform, physically fit men who you know could protect you from a mugger or a burglar without batting an eyelash. And I've been attracted to men who serve their country. But at the same time I knew that I didn't want to marry a Special Forces guy like my dad, because then I would end up never seeing him and being lonely and sneaking around having affairs and stuff. So I always tended to date military guys who were in the more normal branches of the military—guys who stayed at home for long periods of time and had jobs which, well, maybe they weren't nine to five, but at least they could sleep in their own beds at night.

"My husband, Tim, is a prime example of my type. He's also a former military officer and a former MP. He was in the Coast Guard. In fact I met him while we were both still in the service, but I never started dating him 'til much later—after we were both out of the service. He wanted the same kind of life that I wanted, and he made a similar career move.

"However, Tim ended up working for the DEA, because he had been involved in drug enforcement while he was in the Coast Guard. Besides being a military man, he is in great shape, and we share the same values. If I had to compare him to my dad, I would say that he is just as strong and just as dedicated, but he lacks the gung-ho, nearly insane need for danger that the Special Forces guys seem to feed on. He's like a tamed-down version of my dad."

So here again with Delphine we find a daughter who had very limited exposure to her dad and filled in the missing pieces with positive attributes that she later sought out in her adult relationships. Delphine was saved from recreating the loneliness her mother experienced because she saw that loneliness. She recognized that her mother was in love with her father and with the self-sacrificing serviceman that he was, but she was able to differentiate the desirable qualities that attracted her mother to her father from the big downside of chronic loneliness that comes with loving such a dedicated soldier.

It is interesting that in the virtual absence of personal interactions with her father, Delphine was able to extrapolate from her mother a pretty complete picture of what marriage to such a man might be. And from this picture, she was able to differentiate the desirable qualities from the undesirable ones. It is almost as though the clarity of her fantasy image of her father was facilitated by the complete absence of any complications that might have arisen if he had actually been present in her life during her childhood and adolescence.

The Path to Recovery

So we see in this chapter that the daughters of fathers who are absent tend to fill in the missing pieces to construct a complete picture of the man for themselves. This picture may be accurate or inaccurate, but more often than not, it is a favorable one. After all, if you need to construct a father based on few data, you might as well construct a good one.

Having constructed this ideal image, these daughters then tend to attempt to fill the void created by their dad's absence by finding a partner who matches up with the image.

Some daughters of absent fathers, like Antonia and Anne, construct only a partial fantasy image of their fathers, and they seek out men who match their father on a few salient characteristics. These daughters run the risk that the partners they select may prove less than ideal, based on characteristics that they never included in the fantasy image of Dad or the search they made based on that image.

Antonia was impetuous in plunging into relationships, and she had rather poor luck in selecting a husband due to unknown factors that were not covered under the criteria of "tall, thin, and a good sense of humor." In contrast, Anne was a bit more careful and looked beyond initial attraction based on her fantasy model of her dad. When Anne did find a man she thought would fill the bill, she had still not considered all of the potentially relevant characteristics of a good partner. But she had rather good luck in her choice of John.

Still other daughters, like Delphine, somehow manage to construct a more complete fantasy to use as a model in seeking a partner, or at least they include in their search criteria some realistic criteria to help them screen out possible sources of dissatisfaction with the partners they choose.

Since the factors that lie behind feelings of attraction are often unconscious, many daughters of absent fathers are not even aware of the extent to which their fantasy construction of their father plays a role in their choice of partners. It may take a friend to point out, "There seems to be a pattern here." But the lesson to be learned here is that if you do feel that your father hasn't been present in your life, you may want to give some thought to the partners to whom you are attracted, and what it is about them that makes them so desirable.

Part Two

The Path to Recovery

Chapter Seven

Assessing the Damage

In reading the life stories in the first six chapters, you may well have recognized some characteristics of your father and your relationship with your father. Was he a disapproving father? Do you suspect that he had a mental illness or personality disorder? Did he abuse drugs or alcohol? Was he abusive, unreliable, or absent? If he is an extreme example of one of the types, you may well have known that there were problems long before you picked up this book. In that case, I hope that reading these stories has done two things for you. First, I hope that they have made it abundantly clear that you aren't alone in your experience with your unavailable father. Many other daughters have had similar relationships. Second, I hope these stories have shown you that broken and inadequate father-daughter relationships are more than just painful at the time. Growing up as the daughter of an unavailable father often leaves lasting scars that affect adult identity, self-esteem, and relationships.

But perhaps your father does not fit neatly into a single type. This is common, because many fathers have multiple problems. Substance-abusing fathers are often verbally, physically, or sexually abusive because drugs and alcohol lower inhibitions and lead men to act out angry, selfish, carnal impulses they might otherwise keep under control. Similarly, men with bipolar disorder frequently act irresponsibly when they're in the manic phase of the illness. They may spend money wildly, disappear for weeks at a time, and gamble. These behaviors also characteristic of fathers who fall in the "unreliable" category.

The fact that unavailable fathers do not always fit neatly into one category tends to muddy the waters for daughters who are attempting to understand what happened. In addition, some unavailable fathers are simply more extreme than others. For example, one disapproving father may dismiss his daughter's accomplishments by simply demonstrating a lack of interest or not showing up on special occasions. Another disapproving father may display his disdain by criticizing her endeavors, insulting her, or demeaning her accomplishments. In this case, disapproval has crossed the line into emotional abuse.

The resulting lack of clarity regarding just what a father's problem was and how serious the problems were can be a problem for adult daughters, because it promotes denial. If your father was the town drunk and he hurt you time after time by abusing your mom, spending the rent at the bar, breaking up the house, and getting arrested for driving under the influence, you might be ashamed or guilty and deny it when a friend tells you your father's an alcoholic and his addiction has left you scarred. Furthermore, you might very well resist any suggestion from this same friend about doing something to fix things up and make your life easier, such as join a peer support group for adult children of alcoholics.

The self-test that follows will help you assess the extent to which your father was unavailable and the way he demonstrated his unavailability. Completing this questionnaire will help you figure out whether your father was unavailable and also will give you a good idea of the nature of his unavailability. This knowledge will help you understand how you may have been damaged and what you might need to do to recover.

The Father-Daughter Relationship
Assessment Questionnaire

There are forty statements in this questionnaire. All you need to do is check the ones that you consider true of your relationship with your father. Don't wait too long to respond; go with your first impression. It should only take five or six minutes to run through the forty statements.

Check If True

1. My father was generally too busy with work to pay any attention to me. _____

2. I think my father would rather I had been a boy. _____

3. My father's behavior was sometimes bizarre. _____

4. My father rarely or never asked me about the things I was interested in. _____

5. My father didn't tell me that he loved me. _____

6. I was afraid to play or to touch things because I thought I would "make a mess" or put things back "out of order." _____

7. My father sometimes broke things that I valued or mistreated my pet. _____

8. There were times when I was afraid to get into the car if my father was driving. _____

9. My father rarely or never hugged me or kissed me. _____

10. My father vacillated between being very high and very low. _____

11. There were times when I had my feelings hurt by my father's insults. _____

12. My father thought that some activities were "just for boys." _____

13. My father made promises that he did not keep. _____

14. My father sometimes hurt me physically. _____

15. My family sometimes ran short of money to pay the bills. _____

16. I often felt that I had to be really nice to everyone in order to be liked. _____

17. When I entered puberty, my father seemed to become less interested in me. _____

18. My father gave me approval only when I got perfect grades in school. _____

19. My father put spending time with his buddies ahead of spending time with me. _____

20. I was afraid of my father's anger. _____

21. My father had one or more other residences where he spent time away from the family. _____

22. My father died before I was twelve years old.   ____

23. My father sometimes did not show up when he said he would.   ____

24. I remember times when I felt embarrassed because people were talking about my father.   ____

25. My father rarely or never told me I was beautiful.   ____

26. I never felt that my father was open to my choice of a friend, a date, or a partner.   ____

27. There were times when I felt uncomfortable because my father touched me in a sexual way.   ____

28. My father did not give me a regular allowance.   ____

29. My father abandoned me.   ____

30. My father never expressed any interest in my friends or social life.   ____

31. My father believed that certain careers were appropriate for women.   ____

32. I often felt that no matter what I did, it would never be enough.   ____

33. I sometimes avoided my father because I knew that he would make nasty comments about me.   ____

34. My father sometimes missed holidays.   ____

35. My father rarely or never came to my activities.   ____

36. My father disappeared for long periods of time.   ____

37. My father was emotionally or physically abusive toward my mother.   ____

38. I remember being afraid that my father would show up drunk in public.   ____

39. My father made sexually explicit jokes or remarks in front of me when I was small.   ____

40. I often felt as though I had to take responsibility for keeping the household together.   ____

To interpret your answers, count up the following totals, and write down the numbers on the lines provided:

Assessment Summary

Number of Items Checked

Overall Unavailability Score

Total number of items checked out of 40 _____

Disapproving Father Score

Total number checked out of the following items:
1, 2, 4, 5, 9, 12, 16, 17, 18, 25, 26, 28, 30, 31, 32, 35

Score (maximum score: 16) _____

Mentally Ill Father Score

Total number checked out of the following items:
3, 6, 10, 16, 24, 36, 40

Score (maximum score: 7) _____

Substance-Abusing Father Score

Total number checked out of the following items:
3, 8, 16, 24, 38, 40

Score (maximum score: 6) _____

Abusive Father Score

Total number checked out of the following items:
7, 8, 11, 14, 20, 24, 27, 33, 37, 39

Score (maximum score: 10) _____

Unreliable Father Score

13, 15, 19, 23, 28, 34, 36

Score (maximum score: 7) _____

Absent Father Score

Total number checked out of the following items:
1, 21, 22, 29, 36

Score (maximum score: 5) _____

Overall Unavailability Score

If you checked more than five of the forty statements, there's a good chance that your father was sufficiently unavailable in one way or another that you may have experienced or may still be experiencing negative consequences in your adult life.

If you checked only around five of these items, you may have never thought of your father or your relationship with your father as a problem. More likely, you just thought of him as possibly a poor dad. Nevertheless, if you checked five or more of these statements, you may have been affected in ways similar to the daughters you've read about in this book. If you checked as many as ten of the forty statements, there is little doubt that your father was unavailable to a degree that warrants further exploration and a conscious act of healing on your part. In the stories I have presented thus far, there is more than sufficient evidence that an unavailable father often fosters adjustment difficulties in his daughter. You may not be aware of the ways in which you have been affected by your unavailable father, and you owe it to yourself to consider it.

Disapproving Father Score

The items in this category can indicate a disapproving father. Not every item is unique to disapproval; several can also indicate other types of unavailable fathers. But if you checked five or more of these items, you may operate on the assumption that your father was disapproving. This means that he failed to show you the type of unconditional love and acceptance that a daughter typically requires in order to grow up feeling good about herself.

If your father failed in this regard, you may now be the kind of woman who tries very hard to please. You may well be quite popular because you work so hard at pleasing people, but you may steadfastly refuse to see yourself as desirable or worthy of approval. You may also have done very well in school and in your career, yet never given yourself much credit for your accomplishments. You may be highly self-critical if you achieve anything less than perfection. You may attribute your successes not to your intelligence, talent, or hard work but rather to external factors such as luck or "being in the right place at the right time."

If your father wanted a boy or held gender-stereotyped attitudes regarding the appropriate activities for a girl, the courses a girl should take, or the careers that were appropriate for young ladies, you may have limited yourself to a circumscribed range of interests, activities, and opportunities. You may have failed to pursue your strongest talents, opting instead for what your father passed down to you as more "appropriate" courses of action.

If your father was threatened by your developing sexuality and disapproved of your choice of friends and dating partners, you may feel unable to make good choices for partners. You may have felt that you had to choose a professional career rather than be, say, a wrangler. Or you may have rebelled and chosen a Hell's Angel just to piss your dad off. If you are gay, a disapproving father may have created major conflict for you. As a result, you may have denied your feelings and tried to partner with a man, creating a relationship destined to failure and frustration for both you and your partner.

Clearly these are all obstacles to the realization of your potential and the establishment of mutually satisfying adult relationships.

Mentally Ill Father Score

The seven items in this category of the Assessment Summary are indicative of one or another form of mental illness. Of course, if your father was a florid schizophrenic or was diagnosed with bipolar personality disorder, you might justifiably point out that you don't need a test to tell you there was a problem. And you would be correct. But not every mental illness is formally diagnosed, and if the mental illness manifests itself when you are a child, you might very well not have understood what was going on.

The statements in this section are designed to provide you with indications of the possibility that your father had a mental illness that made him unavailable to you. Item 6, "I was afraid to play or to touch things," would be expected to be checked by the daughter of a father likely to have an obsessive-compulsive personality disorder. These fathers tend to inhibit the explorations and experimentation of their very young children and stifle the spontaneity of older children. These daughters often become fearful adults— women who are afraid to let themselves go and enjoy life.

Do you sometimes feel that you lack spontaneity? Are there activities that you think you might enjoy that you have never tried just because you wish to remain in your established comfort zone? Are you yourself ever overly concerned with neatness? Do friends and family members ever suggest that you loosen up and enjoy life? These issues often characterize adult daughters of fathers who were obsessive compulsives.

Item 10, "My father vacillated between being very high and being very low," and item 36, "My father disappeared for long periods of time," are often indicative of bipolar personality disorder. Fathers with this disorder are often morose and sullen when they're at home during a depressed period, and then they cycle into a manic episode, during which they might run off to a place like Las Vegas and dissipate the family savings.

The daughter of a father with a bipolar disorder finds that her father is unavailable during both the depressive and the manic phases of the illness. When he is depressed, he is uncommunicative. When he is manic, there's a good chance that he isn't listening to anyone else, or he's just plain gone. The daughters of bipolar fathers experience both embarrassment and insecurity: they don't want friends to see their father depressed, and they don't want friends to know when he has run off. They also suffer from observing the impact of their father's illness on their mother, who may well be forced to take the full responsibility for the welfare of the family because she never knows when her husband will disappear.

Item 3, "My father's behavior was sometimes bizarre," and item 24, "I remember times when I felt embarrassed because people were talking about my father," could indicate a father with mental illness. For example, daughters of fathers who have schizophrenia experience both social anxiety and insecurity. Their problems are exacerbated by the fact that their mother is frequently required to devote a great deal of energy to managing her husband's illness, leaving her too depleted to devote much time and energy to her daughter. Some daughters of fathers with schizophrenia also fear that they will inherit the condition, since some research indicates that it can run in the family.

The other two items that count toward the mental illness score are item 16, "I often felt that I had to be really nice to everyone in order to be liked," and item 40, "I often felt as though I had to take responsibility for keeping the household together." These items reflect the stigma attached to mental illness, which a daughter may feel rubs off on her, and the fact that her mom is wrapped up with her dad's illness, leaving household chores and the care of any younger siblings to her daughter.

Substance-Abusing Father Score

The items counted in this section are indications of a substance-abusing father. If you checked more than two of these, you should give this issue some thought.

There's a good deal of overlap between the statements in the assessment that indicate mental illness and those that indicate substance abuse. This is partly because mentally ill individuals and substance-abusing individuals engage in some of the same behaviors. For example, bizarre and delusional behavior characteristic of people with schizophrenia are also characteristic of those with advanced alcoholism and men under the influence of hallucinogens. It is also partly because many mentally ill men use alcohol to self-medicate. This is a common but really bad strategy, because alcohol is a depressant and tends to worsen psychiatric symptoms.

The overlap is due in part as well to the similarity of effects of the two conditions on daughters. For example, a father with schizophrenia and one with alcoholism might be equally embarrassing to their daughters. And the wife of a man with either of these diseases might have to devote similar amounts of their time and effort to care for her husband, leaving little energy for the children.

A substance-abusing father will most likely behave in a manner that makes it difficult or impossible for his daughter to have a normal childhood. If you grew up in a home where chaos was the norm, you may have never formed a clear idea about what life "should be" like. You may have gone through a large portion of your life not recognizing that it's unusual and undesirable for the home to be in disarray, the father to be passed out on the couch instead of at work, the refrigerator empty, and the telephone turned off for nonpayment. You may have dated or even married a substance abuser without ever giving serious thought to whether this was a problem. Or you may have recognized that the substance abuse was a problem and tried your best as a child to either "fix it" or to insulate yourself from its effects. In this case, your childhood efforts to cope with your father's substance abuse have probably determined to a great degree the type of adult woman you have become.

Volumes have been written about the effects of a father's substance abuse on his adult children. If a daughter is the oldest child in the family, she frequently assumes significant responsibility prematurely, taking charge of cooking and cleaning and caring for younger siblings. Because she is embarrassed for the family by her father's drunkenness, she often feels compelled to be a high achiever in school because she thinks that someone must set an example to maintain whatever shred of dignity remains for the family. Thus, the firstborn becomes the "responsible one." She is focused on responsibilities at home and in school. She has little time for a social life and little time to spend imagining possibilities for the future. She is likely to choose a fairly predictable career path, simply because she hasn't allowed herself the luxury of exploring new horizons or taking chances on less predictable areas of endeavor.

Second-born daughters of substance abusers typically have the problem that the oldest child has already assumed the role of the most responsible. No matter how responsible a second-born daughter might be, she can never supplant her older sibling from this role. Under these circumstances, the second daughter of a father with alcoholism often chooses a rebel role. She may become a substance abuser herself. She may act out in other ways, including truancy, delinquent behavior, premature sexuality, or promiscuity. She will also frequently marry someone just like her father—another substance abuser.

Abusive Father Score

The items in this section of the Assessment Summary are indicative of abusive fathers. Any reader who checks three or more of these items was certainly abused by her father, and in some cases, checking a single item is enough to establish that abuse occurred.

The possibility that your father abused you emotionally is indicated by your checking any of five items: item 7, "My father sometimes broke things that I valued or mistreated my pet"; item 11, "There were times when I had my feelings hurt by my father's insults"; item 20, "I was afraid of my father's anger"; item 33, "I sometimes avoided my father because I knew he would make nasty comments about me"; or item 37, "My father was emotionally or physically abusive toward my mother."

The emotional abuse perpetrated by a father who constantly insults and demeans his daughter is pretty obvious. The other items indicating emotional abuse are less clear. We don't ordinarily think of an abusive father as taking his anger out on his daughter by hurting or destroying something that she loves, but the fact is that abusive men often do so. In some cases, they are afraid that if they attack their victim physically, they might be arrested. If they destroy her favorite stuffed animal or kill her pet, however, there will probably be no outside repercussions. In addition, emotional abuse may be secondary in nature: a daughter who sees her father verbally, physically, or sexually assaulting her mother will be damaged psychologically as surely as she would be damaged if the assaults were made on her.

Physical abuse is indicated by item 14, "My father sometimes hurt me physically." Sexual abuse is indicated by item 27, "There were times when I felt uncomfortable because my father touched me in a sexual way," and item 39, "My father made sexually explicit jokes or remarks in front of me when I was small."

Emotional abuse, physical abuse, and sexual abuse experienced in childhood can leave scars that can last a lifetime. Daughters who are insulted and ridiculed by their fathers on a routine basis will likely develop very poor self-concepts. After all, if you are told often enough that you are worthless, the chances are pretty good that eventually you'll come to believe that this is true.

Even if you recognize that objectively you have good looks and talent, you are likely to assume that there must be something wrong with you or your father wouldn't treat you this way. As an adult, maintaining an unconscious belief that you are not very lovable or valuable will likely make you socially anxious. You may simply withdraw from social interactions, or you may feel self-conscious and nervous on any occasion when you feel that you are on display and subject to the judgments of others.

In addition, women whose fathers insult them when they are young, like Margaret in Chapter Four, often come to feel that people in general, and men in particular, are a source not of love and affection but rather of ridicule and pain. The verbal abuse that Margaret experienced from her father led her to develop an attachment disorder that has not allowed her to form a serious committed relationship with a man.

The lesson Margaret learned in childhood made perfect sense then. She told herself, "Don't get close to father, or he will insult you, hurt your feelings, and make you feel worthless." As an adult, her avoidant reaction to men persists, but now it is dysfunctional. Her inability to get close to a man and allow herself to become vulnerable results in the inevitable loss of any possibility for rewarding love relationships.

If your father was emotionally abusive to you, then it is quite likely that you, like Margaret, have difficulty allowing yourself to become close to others. This is truly a limiting situation that can take away the most rewarding aspects of living: those derived from forming deep, mutually rewarding relationships. If you now feel that your father was emotionally abusive, you need to give some thought to how it has affected your relationships. You may need to do some work to develop the capacity to take the risk of getting close.

Daughters who are physically or sexually abused by their fathers generally suffer from the symptoms of posttraumatic stress disorder as adults. They may exhibit startle responses to loud noises or angry shouts. They may experience chronic anxiety and fearfulness. They may feel constantly threatened, and they may be socially withdrawn. They may feel helpless and ineffectual, due to the powerlessness they experienced while being abused. They may manifest sudden outbursts of suppressed rage and experience various forms of sexual dysfunction.

Fortunately, in recent years much attention has been devoted within the mental health community to issues related to symptoms of PTSD, and many resources are available to help relieve the symptoms of these problems. I discuss some of the options in the next chapter.

Unreliable Father Score

The items in section 6 of the Assessment Summary are indications of a father who is unreliable. Generally these men are simply selfish, immature, and self-absorbed. They never assume the responsibility of becoming a father. They fail to keep promises (item 13), they think nothing of spending time with their buddies at the expense of spending time with their children (item 19), they don't show up when they have said that they will (item 23), they are absent when they should be home for an important holiday (item 34), and they disappear for long periods of time to pursue personal interests (item 36). They are also irresponsible financially, even to the point that the family "sometimes ran short of money" (item 15) or they did not provide the children with a regular allowance (item 28).

If you checked three of more of the seven items in this group, it's likely that your father was sufficiently unreliable as to undermine any sense of security in your family. The failure to feel secure as a child may have made you overly concerned with keeping your world safe as an adult. You may be extremely cautious, possibly even miserly, regarding finances.

In addition, you may carry into adulthood the idea that men in general cannot be depended on for anything. This may leave you apprehensive regarding the possibility of becoming close to and possibly someday marrying any man. You may anticipate only disappointment from men, and don't assume the possibility of a mutual relationship in which both parties contribute and take care of each other.

An unreliable father may be particularly frustrating for a daughter because these fathers are not necessarily cold or unloving. If you had such a father, you may have loved him to death and really wanted him to be home for Christmas Eve, but this only made it more painful when he didn't show up.

If you have concluded that you had such a father and that he has adversely affected your ability to feel secure in your adult relationships, there is hope. This hope lies in taking the risk of forging connections and making commitments, so that over time, you can be convinced that there are individuals who can be depended on to show up and contribute their fair share to the relationship. We consider such efforts in more detail in the following chapter.

Absent Father Score

A father who is physically absent cannot provide his daughter with unconditional love and validation. Nor can he give her a sense of security and the conviction that people are dependable. A young child doesn't understand why her father is missing. She only knows that he is gone.

The items in the final section of the Assessment Summary all concern the daughter's perception of her father as simply missing. A father may be absent because he died. If you checked item 22 ("My father died before I was twelve") and no other item in this group, you could still experience difficulties in adulthood because he was gone. The age chosen for the question is to some extent open to question. Certainly adolescent daughters whose fathers die while they are in high school or college may have a very difficult time adjusting to the loss. But at least they are old enough to understand death. A daughter under twelve years old may not understand that death is beyond her control. She may even experience unconscious feelings of guilt. Furthermore, when she does reach adulthood, her father will have been gone for some time. This will allow her the latitude to construct a fantasy father, as Antonia did, whom she can then seek for the rest of her life.

Fathers can be physically absent for reasons other than death. They may be so wound up in their work that they are never home (item 1). For example, a father may be a military officer who is stationed overseas for long periods of time, as in the case of Delphine. Some men have jobs that divide their time between two or three different locations. Thus, item 21 states, "My father had one or more other residences where he spent time away from the family." In such circumstances, the father may be away ostensibly because he is working to earn a good living for his family. This might be the truth, or it might really be that he has another life there. It doesn't matter. If he is gone, his intention would be less important to a child than the fact of his physical absence.

A daughter may also feel that her father has abandoned her (item 29). This may be the result of a teenage pregnancy, or it may be the result of a bad divorce after which a spiteful mother drives her former husband away. From the point of view of a young daughter, the reason for her father's absence is less important than the perception of being abandoned. If you checked this one item and you believe that your father abandoned you, then you have quite likely experienced some emotional damage. Young girls inevitably wonder what it was about them that caused their dad to walk away.

Using the Results of the Father-Daughter Assessment

I hope that the Father-Daughter Assessment has helped you to determine whether your father was unavailable and, if so, how his unavailability may have affected your adjustment and satisfaction with life as a child and as an adult. I also hope that the stories presented in Part One of this book have made it clear that the daughters of unavailable fathers can be resilient and successful. Sometimes the daughters of unavailable fathers are able to rise above the deprivations of their childhood spontaneously, or through the good fortune of finding friends or a special partner who helps to repair the damage and open new doors. Sometimes, however, a daughter of an unavailable father must take some specific action aimed at achieving recovery. I consider such efforts to achieve recovery in the next chapter.

Chapter Eight

The Path to Recovery

I end this book with ideas for doing work that is necessary for you to overcome the legacy of the past and move forward into a brighter future unencumbered by the baggage left behind by your father's failures. In providing these guidelines, I do not want to convey the idea that all the effects of your unavailable father can be wholly eliminated. However, there is much that you can do to ameliorate the impact of an unavailable father, and taking an active role in striving to overcome the past will certainly improve your mood and outlook on life.

Steps Along the Path

Although there are different types of unavailable fathers who leave their daughters with very different types of problems, there is only one path to recovery. As the daughter of an unavailable father, you must

- Understand what really happened to you as a child
- Determine the attitudes and behaviors that you developed back then in order to explain his failures and protect yourself
- Figure out which of these attitudes and behaviors you have carried into adulthood
- Recognize how these attitudes and behaviors have limited you in the past and may still be limiting your happiness
- Substitute new attitudes and behaviors that expand your possibilities for happiness for these ineffective ones

- Assess the impact of these new attitudes and behaviors on your life now
- Modify and refine these new attitudes and behaviors so as to achieve the best possible outcomes

Sounds pretty simple, right? Well, yes, but only in theory. To follow this path through to its conclusion in a brighter, happier future may require hard work, courage, and even the capacity to endure considerable discomfort or even pain. But I believe that it is worth it. The sections of this chapter that follow describe each of these steps along the path in some detail. They indicate how to take each step, the difficulties associated with each step, and the possible positive outcomes.

These steps are a general outline. Some readers will have already completed or at least have a pretty good idea regarding some of them. Still, it is a good idea to at least consider them in order, because giving careful thought and effort to each step may well reveal important events or ideas that are not immediately apparent to you.

Understand What Really Happened to You as a Child

Some of you will think that you know damned good and well what happened. Like Billie, it may be clear to you that your dad really wanted a boy. Like Cora, you may be quite certain that your dad was simply nuts. Like Carey, you may know (along with the entire town) that your father was a drunk. Like Katie, you may remember quite well the times that he hit you. Okay. But you could still benefit from some research, because the circumstances surrounding these certainties may be less clear.

Remember that you were a child. You might remember the sad feeling that came when your dad expressed no interest in your games, and you may remember that you were embarrassed when the kids in school talked behind your back. But you may not have a very clear idea of how these events worked themselves out. Did you become depressed? Did you become shy and anxious? You must understand these particulars to understand how you were affected.

Or you might not have a very good idea at all regarding what your father did or did not do that now causes you to have a sense that something wasn't right or he really didn't treat you very well. In either case, you owe it to yourself to get as much information as you can about your father and your relationship with your father when you were young.

So what can you do? If your father is still alive and still in touch, you can go straight to the source. Start by asking him. Of course, this can be easy or difficult, depending on your relationship with him now. You may need some support from a friend, your significant other, or fellow members in a support group to gather up the courage to undertake this task.

Many adults who perceive themselves as products of difficult circumstances during childhood become members of peer groups in which they can receive support and information. There are groups for adult children of alcoholics, adult children of the mentally ill, adults who were abused as children, and adults who lost one or both parents at an early age. These groups are helpful for many people, and I encourage you to consider joining one if you think this might be helpful. You might consider joining a general psychotherapy group as well or even entering therapy. All of these vehicles can be helpful. But none of them is required in order for you to proceed along the path to recovery that I have outlined here.

Talk to Your Father

So how do you go approach your father? First, you *do not* approach him in anger. When you seek a meeting with your father to revisit your childhood, don't think of it as a confrontation. Implicit in that word is that this is a quarrel, and a person on the defensive is rarely ready to talk. Try to look it as a fact-finding mission. If you are seething with anger that you can't get under control, try asking someone else to listen to what you plan to say to your father.

Sometimes running through the feelings that you wish to get off your chest will help you to keep focused and keep your angry feelings under control when you actually talk with your father.

When you do meet with him, don't begin by asking him to explain why he hurt you the way he did. That won't get you very far. Instead, tell him that you are trying to get a sense of where you came from and how you ended up where you are. Then ask him what he remembers about your childhood. This should help to minimize his defensiveness, and it will allow him to begin speaking about areas where he feels most comfortable. Later in your conversation, you can ask him to tell you more about some of the things that he has mentioned, and perhaps you can even steer him in the direction of your relationship with him and how he views himself as a father.

Intersperse any inquiries of this nature with questions about other family members and questions about what he was doing at the time. These questions will make it less obvious that the agenda is really how he failed you. In addition, these more neutral questions may also yield some important facts about the family's situation during your childhood that might help to explain his behavior toward you. For example, you might learn that he was preoccupied for a good part of your childhood because his business was on the rocks, or that he was hurting because he and your mother were going through a particularly difficult period in their marriage. Information such as this might not justify the way he treated you, but it might help you to understand a little better the pressures that he may have been under. It might help you to forgive. If this is the case, you may well find that increasing your understanding of what happened facilitates your own healing.

Talk to Other Family Members

Don't stop with your father. Even if you succeed in minimizing his defensiveness during your discussion, his memories will still be biased. It is only natural that he would see himself and his actions in the best light possible. Ask your mom and other relatives to tell you what they remember about your childhood and your relationship with your father as well. This will give you information derived from several different perspectives. You can compare the reports and use them to piece together the best picture possible of what happened.

These investigations should help you to cut through the defenses that you may have built to shield yourself from the reality of your father's failures. You should find that you are able to rid yourself of past denial. When you say, "Daddy wasn't a drunk. He was just tired when he got home and the liquor hit him hard," or "He was only violent when my mother drove him to it," you're hiding the truth.

In childhood it feels safer to keep things hidden from outsiders— and from yourself. But when the pattern persists into adulthood, it allows you to deny the way things were. You can't change the things you refuse to see. Gathering data from firsthand witnesses should make it much easier for you to perceive your father's actions accurately and label them accordingly.

Determine the Attitudes and Behaviors That You Developed Back Then in Order to Explain His Failures and Protect Yourself

Step 2 along the path to recovery is to get a good picture of how you responded to your father's unavailability at the time. In your discussions with firsthand witnesses, make sure that you ask what they remember about you during this period. Ask them if they think you were well adjusted or instead behaved strangely or appeared distressed. If they say that you seemed unhappy or distressed, ask them if they have any ideas about why that might be. Don't ask leading questions or put words in their mouths. Just ask them what they saw and how they interpreted it at the time.

As you investigate your past relationship with your father, you will likely remember certain events and situations in which you can also recall what you did in response to his behavior. Can you remember feeling disappointed and angry when he told you that he couldn't spend time with your or attend your school play? Can you remember avoiding him because you feared he would be critical or make demeaning comments about you? Can you remember thinking that if you could only get all A's on your report card, he might give you some praise? Can you remember thinking that all this craziness with your dad was just too hard on your mother, and you needed to help her out by taking over some of the household chores? Can you remember avoiding schoolmates because you thought they might be saying demeaning things about your father? Can you remember refraining from asking friends over to your house because you never knew whether your dad would be angry, or drunk, or crazy? Write down all these responses so that you won't forget them. Keep this list for future reference.

Observe and Read About Other Children's Lives

While you are gathering information from others and reflecting on your responses during childhood, you might well benefit from considering your own children or other children who are around the same age as you were when your father was failing you. Something as simple as going to a playground and watching young children at play will remind you of how fragile and vulnerable they are. This may help you to appreciate just how painful it may have been for you to endure your father's lack of interest, criticism, or abuse.

You might also benefit from reading about the experiences of other children in similar circumstances. Of course, you have already done a bit of that by reading the first part of this book, but there are many more sources available. Have you read Dickens? If not, reading *David Copperfield* or *Oliver Twist* might help you to appreciate further the vulnerability of children in difficult circumstances.

Keep in mind that you are a survivor. Although you may have been damaged by your father's unavailability, you have survived. This means that you have toughened yourself and defended against the hurt. In so doing, you have most likely minimized in your mind the pain and insults you experienced. It may be necessary for you to look beneath the defenses that are already in place in order to fully appreciate what you went through. You are older now, and you should be able to do this. It may not be easy, but it is important.

Talk to Others About What You're Finding Out

For the same reason, you might very well benefit from sharing your explorations with someone who has had similar experiences. Here again the possibility of participating in a peer support group comes to mind, but a formal group is not required. Sharing some of your experiences with any caring friend or relative will help to give you a different perspective on what you experienced and how you responded. The chances are that the reactions of such a supporter will make it clear to you that what you experienced was indeed hurtful, and how you responded was quite understandable under the circumstances.

Figure Out Which of These Attitudes and Behaviors You Have Carried into Adulthood

At this point along the path, you may have a pretty good idea of what your father failed to do (or did) that hurt you, and how you responded in order to cope with his failure. You understand that the things you did at that time made sense: you sought to protect yourself, and perhaps you sought to protect your mom as well.

So you began to think and act in ways that most other children your age didn't. You avoided socializing because you weren't sure anyone would like you. Why should they? Your father didn't. You tried hard to be perfect in school—not just good but perfect. Maybe then you could get your father to tell you that you were worth something. You avoided after-school activities so that you could go home and help with the laundry and cleaning. You wanted to get these things finished before your mom got home from work. This was important, because the family couldn't depend on your dad to pay the rent or buy the groceries. And maybe you didn't date because you were far more afraid of men than interested in getting close to them.

Whatever coping responses you used during the previous step along the path to recovery, the chances are that at the time, they represented reasonable and even effective defenses against the hurt you were experiencing at the hands of your unavailable father. But are you still responding to people as you did then? And are these responses working for you now?

Once people begin to behave in a certain manner, they are likely to continue to do so. This is particularly true about behaviors learned during childhood and behaviors learned under stress. But the problem is that many of the attitudes and behaviors that we adopted because of our fathers' failures are as dysfunctional to us as adults as they were useful to us as children.

Repeating Childhood Responses That Don't Work

The next step in the path to recovery is to take that list you made of your childhood responses to your father's unavailability, and consider each item. You will be asking yourself whether the response you learned then has been carried into your adult life.

If you avoided social contact as an adolescent because you didn't feel attractive or because you felt embarrassed about the scene at home, do you find that you still experience social anxiety? Do you still worry about whether your clothes are appropriate or whether your home is presentable? If you hid at the sound of an angry voice when you were a child because you were afraid that your father would come and yell at you or hit you, do you still fall apart whenever someone raises his voice? If you felt "dirty" because your stepfather made a habit of fondling your bottom or breasts, do you now find yourself feeling uptight in sexual encounters? If you were afraid to touch anything in your house because your father was obsessive-compulsive and blew up when something was left out of place, do you now find that you yourself are compulsively neat and clean?

What you need to do is to produce your own list of attitudes and behaviors that you clearly recognize as resulting directly from childhood defensive coping responses. If you are like most of my patients and most of the women with whom I have discussed this topic, there is a good chance that you will find a nearly perfect one-to-one correspondence between defensive strategies that you adopted as a child and attitudes and behaviors that you have carried over into your adult life.

Recognize How These Attitudes and Behaviors Have Limited You in the Past and May Still Be Limiting Your Happiness

The fourth step along the path to recovery is to recognize the dysfunctional nature of the attitudes and the defensive behaviors that you have carried over from your childhood relationship with your father to your adult relationships.

It should not be surprising to you that this would be an important step toward recovery, since that's what millions of people are trying to do when they get involved in psychotherapy. Isn't the main goal of most therapy to figure out how things we learned when we were children are screwing us up today?

So at this point along the path, you are going to look at each attitude and behavior pattern that you have identified as carried over from the failed relationship with your dad and analyze that attitude or behavior to figure out what role it plays for you now.

You can begin this undertaking by making and considering a list of attitudes you developed then that are destructive now, including all of the defensive behaviors you learned then that prevent you from experiencing life to the fullest extent possible right now.

Even a woman who has always underestimated her intelligence, wit, and physical attractiveness is likely to discern that these feelings inhibit her ability to meet and form relationships with people who could contribute to her happiness. Even a woman who has learned to expect disappointment in relationships can understand that such expectations can become self-fulfilling prophecies.

But don't stop with yourself and your own impressions of how the old attitudes and defensive behaviors are dysfunctional now. Ask your family, your friends, your colleagues, your lover. You don't even have to ask them in the context of your relationship with your father. You can simply tell them that you have embarked on a self-improvement plan and need them to help you identify any attitudes or habits that you have that they think might be holding you back from achieving your full potential personally, professionally, or socially. You can write down their responses and match them up with your list of carried-over behaviors later. You should also consider each attitude and behavior they mention, whether you can match it with a carried-over attitude or behavior of not.

Consider each attitude or behavior that you identify in this manner. Think through what you are doing that is limiting you, and try to come up with an alternative way of thinking or behaving for each one. It is usually not too difficult to identify and articulate behaviors that would be better than the dysfunctional carry-over attitudes and behaviors.

Substitute New Attitudes and Behaviors That Expand Your Possibilities for Happiness for These Ineffective Ones

Now here comes the hard part: changing the way you think and behave. This will require a good deal of work and perhaps a substantial amount of courage.

Old ideas about who we are, what we're worth, and what we can do are not easy to change. New behaviors that you need to put into practice are often very scary. For example, if you are shy and inhibited socially, you will need to learn how to be more outgoing about socializing. This is obviously a difficult order, because you have been acting shy for a long time and because you have been acting that way because you have been apprehensive about how people might respond to you. You will be asking yourself to take a big risk.

Thinking Differently About Yourself

But let's put first things first: your attitudes toward yourself. The daughters of unavailable fathers typically have rather poor self-concepts. So no matter how talented, hard working, and attractive you may be by any objective standard, you very likely see yourself as having little or no talent, not working hard enough, and plain looking. You need to change these self-concepts.

A good way to begin to think differently about yourself is to conduct a review of your accomplishments and successes. Rethink your academic career. How well did you do in school? How did your grades compare to those of others? How did you perform on standardized exams? Did you receive any academic honors? Try to think of yourself not in terms of how far your academic career was from perfect, but rather how much better you did than most other people.

Rethink your work or career. What is your profession? Do you help others? Do you perform a valuable service to the community? How successful are you in relation to others in that profession? How much do you earn? What awards have you received?

Rethink your appearance. Take a really good look in the mirror and ask yourself whether you aren't really pretty attractive. Are you in good physical shape? Do people compliment you on your looks or the way you dress?

Go back and read whatever letters of recommendation have been written for you over the course of your lifetime. Do they say good things? Why shouldn't you believe them? Ask yourself if you would tend to view yourself in such negative terms if your father hadn't imparted the message to you as a child that he didn't love you or consider you beautiful.

A personal review of what you have accomplished will begin to help you question your assumption that you have little about you that is worthy or attractive. However, this is only a first step, because you have become used to minimizing your positives and maximizing your negatives. Therefore, you must supplement your own fresh look at yourself with information from others. A good way to alter negative self-perceptions is to arrange for frequent feedback from trusted and respected sources who will testify to the fact that you are in fact worthy and desirable. Don't hesitate to ask for validation from friends and family.

Tell them flat-out that you think you have a problem with self-concept and need them to reinforce your worth. You will likely be pleasantly surprised by their responses. In many cases, women who seek help to bolster their self-concepts find that those they ask for help are in full agreement that they have undervalued their worth, and they are willing and ready to help.

In addition, give some thought to the times in your life when someone has approached you for companionship or romance. Even if you held them off, deflected their advances, or refused to allow a serious relationship to develop, such instances certainly suggest that you are worthy of another's interest or attractive. Daughters of unavailable fathers often find ways to extricate themselves from involvements before they progress to the point where there is a real connection. After all, a connection carries with it the potential to be hurt, left, or abandoned. But this is just another example of how the defenses you developed then are hurting you now. Take the advances of others at face value. They found you attractive.

Taking Action

Now comes the hard part. You can do a great deal to help you feel better about yourself, but the real test lies in your actions. You need to discard the old, dysfunctional patterns of behavior that have limited you and replace them with new alternative behaviors that will expand your possibilities for greater satisfaction with your life. In the previous step along the path, you have already come up with a list of the alternative behaviors. Now you must put them into practice.

Let's assume for now that as an adolescent, you responded to your father's indifference by becoming a compulsive overachiever.

Let's further assume that the poor self-concept you developed as a result of his failure to validate you or recognize your accomplishments has made you one of those women who never gives herself credit for her accomplishments and doesn't think of herself as interesting or attractive.

Say you've gone through high school, college, and law school with near-perfect grades, and you've become head counsel for a major environmental defense fund. You've won important cases, appeared on television, received some significant awards honoring your work, and met many interesting and attractive people. But your personal life stinks. You spend sixty hours a week at work, never derive any real gratification from the awards you have been receiving, and never become involved more than superficially with any of the potential friends or love interests who cross your path on a daily basis.

Let's assume further that you have done your homework, and you now understand that you are still thinking and acting the way you did in high school. Let's further assume that you have identified and listed a number of specific beliefs and behaviors that may have protected you then but are ruining your life now. For the sake of argument, let's say that you have said to yourself that, among other things: "I have to work less and allow myself the luxury of free time to broaden my horizons, relax, and enjoy life" and "I have to become more sociable, not in the sense of 'Hello. How are you?' but in the sense of being open to the possibility of forming real friendships and close personal relationships." Identifying these new behaviors is great, but now you must actually do these things. This is the hard part.

Do you have any idea how hard it is for a woman who has spent a life being a workaholic to implement her plan to take time off to enjoy herself? Do you have any idea how hard it is for a woman who has always anxiously avoided close personal relationships to open up and seek out significant involvements? The answers to these questions are obvious. Implementing these new behaviors is very, very difficult. It means breaking old habits and taking risks.

Taking the Time

Whether you're a big success in your career or at a middling level of struggle and survival in today's tough economy, you may have trouble overcoming the entrenched habit of working all the time. For example, you may need to force yourself to leave work on time. This can be difficult if you've always organized your workday on the assumption that it is fourteen or sixteen hours long. So you will need to plan a whole new work schedule. You will need to stop agreeing to have meetings at 6:00 P.M. and on Saturdays. You will need to delegate the legal research work that you have always done yourself to others. You will need to force yourself to leave the comfort zone of your office and go home at night.

Then you will need to fill the space left by quitting work on time. What do you do when you get home? Do you have any interests or hobbies that you can pursue during these newly freed hours? What about going out? For many workaholics who are trying to gain a balance between work and play, the task is difficult as much because they don't know how to play as it is because they don't know how to stop work. You may have to seek out avenues for enjoyment. You may have to do research to discover things other than work that you really want to do.

And what about the second goal of socializing and making yourself open to the possibility of close relationships? This goal also requires breaking old habits. You will need to learn how to convey the idea that "I'm approachable" rather than the idea that "I am much more comfortable if we maintain a distance." You will need to learn how to approach people. If someone asks you to lunch or out on a date, you will have to learn how to bite your tongue when your automatic excuse tries to pop out. You may well be so programmed to avoid exposing yourself socially that you find yourself literally saying no at the same time that you are thinking how great it might be to say, "Yes, of course."

Regardless of the specific behaviors in question, the task is difficult, because it means unlearning one set of habitual responses and learning something new to take their place. The task will most likely require planning, practice, and courage. You might need to ask a friend to rehearse dating skills with you. You might need to learn how to flirt. And, of course, you will need to screw up your courage, because opening up socially carries with it the risk of disappointment and rejection, which is what you feared in the first place, back then.

Don't hesitate to take active steps to implement your goals. You might find that you need a travel consultant to help you actually plan a vacation. You might need to hire a professional dating coach, a female version of the Will Smith character in the movie *Hitch*. You might need to join some clubs or organizations. These are great because they not only provide opportunities to engage in interesting activities but also facilitate meeting new people. You may have many acquaintances from your work, but it might be refreshing to meet some folks who are different. If meeting people is a problem, you might join a dating service or go online to meet people through several well-organized Internet resources now in operation.

The opening-up portion of this goal is another issue. When it comes to sharing your feelings and your hopes for the future with someone else, a different level of training may be required and a new level of risk taking. Here you might really need to ask for help from a friend (which, of course, may itself seem risky). You might want to be in a support group in which you can share these concerns with others who have struggled with the same issues. You might even want to get some counseling. But mainly you will need to be courageous. You can do it. You are worth the effort. You are worth the risk.

Of course, the examples I've given pertain to efforts to implement one specific goal for implementing a new behavior to replace an old dysfunctional one: the goal of socializing and opening up. Your list may include this goal, but it may include a dozen others that are quite different. In fact, the specific goal doesn't matter because the principle is the same. Implementation is often very difficult, and you must be prepared to pull out all the stops to succeed.

Assess the Impact of These New Attitudes and Behaviors on Your Life Now

You've now identified and thrown out negative attitudes. You've also made the effort and shown the courage to put into practice some very new behaviors. Now a large question remains: How are these new ideas and these new behaviors working for you? The chances are the answer to this question will be something like, "Some of them are working, and some of them have really backfired."

Suppose that you have succeeded in destroying the belief that you are untalented and unattractive. Good. Suppose you have attempted to supplant these ideas with the idea that you are talented and attractive. Also good. And suppose that you have gone out into the world and tried to act as a talented, attractive woman might. Only now you encounter some problems. You take painting or fly-fishing lessons, for example, and you fully expect that you will be very good at this, because, after all, you have just finished a process of convincing yourself that you are talented. But you find that you are not so good at painting or fly fishing. In fact, you are not really sure that you even like painting or fly fishing. Welcome to the world.

Women who have made it a habit to defend themselves by focusing their skills and energy on a career at which they excel are likely to have no idea whatsoever about their real skills. You may try out some new activities and find that they are not for you. At this point, it is very important not to give up on yourself and revert to your old attitudes and habits. When you begin to implement new behaviors, you're like a child starting at square one. It is almost as if you put yourself back in time to the point where your father's failures caused you to get off course. But this was during your childhood and adolescence—the time in life when most young women try out different roles to see what they like and what they are good at. Your early defensive retreat in response to your father's unavailability has led you to miss out on this period of exploration and reality testing. So, better late than never, you need to do it now. Therefore, you must allow yourself the latitude to fail at some things and find out that some things you thought might be exciting are really not so exciting at all. And throughout the entire process, you need to give yourself the same unconditional support that you needed then from your father but did not get.

Let's consider another example. Suppose your unavailable father was a handsome, intelligent, witty man but paid no attention to you. Let's further suppose that in the course of walking down the steps to recovery you have ascertained that you (like Deborah in our stories) have always sought out men who remind you of the father who would not give himself to you. And seeking out men who fit this description never worked. So you resolved to open yourself up to the possibility of socializing with men who are very different.

Perhaps you said to yourself, "Let's try out a lifeguard or a tennis pro and see how that works." The truth is that there is no guarantee at all that the lifeguard will be an improvement. You need to be open to new possibilities, but you also have to realize that these are just possibilities. You cannot assume that the first new possibility you try will be the answer to all your problems.

You may find that after experimenting, you don't like being a flirt, you are not fond of skydiving, and you are not bisexual. That's all okay. You need to give yourself the chance to learn the things about yourself that your relationship with your father kept you from learning back then. Try to relax. Give yourself time. Hang out with other people who are trying to discover their way in the world. Enjoy the new behaviors that work well for you, and learn from the ones that don't work out as well. It's all good. It's all a part of your path to recovery.

Modify and Refine These New Attitudes and Behaviors so as to Achieve the Best Possible Outcomes

The final step is to fine-tune your new attitudes and behaviors. When you try something new, you may need to reframe the template you use for evaluating the endeavor.

Far too often, daughters of unavailable fathers have the notion that they must be very good at something in order for it to work. Similarly, they may assume that a new relationship must be perfect in order to be good. But this is simply wrong. There are many women out there who are not particularly intelligent or talented or beautiful who nevertheless have a great deal of fun and consider their lives quite meaningful.

The lesson here is simple: just because you are not the best fly-caster who ever held a rod doesn't mean that you can't enjoy the fishing, or the stream, or a sunny day. And just because the lifeguard is not your ideal life partner doesn't mean that you can't have a good time on the beach.

When children are growing up and trying out new experiences, they learn over time that the answers to their questions are not always black and white. You are not always smart or stupid, talented or untalented, desirable or undesirable. Your father may well have given you the message that you are stupid and untalented and unattractive. You may have responded by trying to show him that you are the perfect scholar or the most talented artist. Or you may have sought to prove him wrong by making it clear to him that every man in town thought you were attractive.

But certainly the truth is that you are quite intelligent, talented, and rather attractive. Or better yet, you are very good in some subjects and not quite so good in others, very talented at some things and not so good at others, and very attractive in some ways but less attractive in others.

I have challenged you to engage in the process of exploring all these possibilities. If you do that, you will have broken the constraints that your father's failures imposed on you. You will have opened up for yourself all the possible rewards that the world can offer.

Resources for Readers

These resources will be helpful to readers who wish to pursue the topic of father-daughter relationships further. I have included a list of general nonfiction works on the topic, as well as a list of pertinent Web sites. I have also included resources that provide information and support services to readers who have identified themselves as falling within one of the specific unavailable-father archetypes. Finally I have suggested some fiction and some movies that deal with the topic of daughters' responses to problematic fathers.

General Nonfiction Works on the Father-Daughter Relationship

Ackerman, R. J. *Perfect Daughters*. Deerfield Beach, Fla.: Health Communications, 2002.

Canfield, J., and Hanson, M. V. *Christian Teens Talk: Their Stories of Support, Inspiration, and Growing Up*. Deerfield Beach, Fla.: Health Communications, 2008.

Canfield, J., Hanson, M. V., Aubry, P., Autio, N. M., and Thieman, L. *Chicken Soup for the Father-Daughter Soul*. Deerfield Beach, Fla.: Health Communications, 2005.

Cosby, B., and Poussaint, A. F. *Come On, People: On the Path from Victims to Victors*. Nashville, Tenn.: Thomas Nelson, 2007.

Cucharria, J. *What All Little Girls Need and What Most Women Never Had—Healthy, Loving Relationships with Their Fathers*. Mustang, Okla.: Tate Publishing, 2005.

Harrison, H. *Father-to-Daughter: Life Lessons on Raising a Girl*. New York: Workman, 2003.

Henslin, E. *You Are Your Father's Daughter*. Nashville, Tenn.: Thomas Nelson, 1994.

Kelly, J. *The Dads and Daughters Togetherness Guide: 54 Fun Activities to Help Build a Great Relationship*. New York: Random House, 2007.

Lang, G. *Why a Daughter Needs a Dad: 100 Reasons*. Naperville, Ill.: Cumberland House, 2007.

Leman, K. *What a Difference a Daddy Makes*. Nashville, Tenn.: Thomas Nelson, 2001.

Maine, M. *Father Hunger: Fathers, Daughters, and Food*. Carlsbad, Calif.: Gurze Books, 1991.

Markovitz, B. *Fathers and Daughters*. New York: Norton, 2005.

Marone, Nicky. *How to Father a Successful Daughter*. New York: Random House, 1998.

Meeker, M., and Meeker, M. *Strong Fathers, Strong Daughters*. New York: Ballantine Books, 2006.

Nielsen. L. "College Daughters' Relationships with Their Fathers: A 15-Year Study." *College Student Journal*, March 2007.

Nielson, L. *Between Fathers and Daughters: Enriching and Rebuilding Your Adult Relationship*. Nashville, Tenn.: Turner Publishing, 2008.

Thomas, P. *Fatherless Daughters: Turning the Pain of Loss into the Power of Forgiveness*. New York: Simon & Schuster, 2009.

Informational Web Sites on Parenting and the Father-Daughter Relationship

www.child-psych.org. See especially N. Lopez-Duran, *Father-Daughter Bond Affects Daughters' Romantic Relationships*.

www.examiner.com. See especially K. Houghton, *Fathers and Daughters—The Relationship*.

www.fathersproject.wordpress.com. A blog about fathers, fatherhood, and everything in-between.

www.life.familyeducation.com/fathers/girls self-esteem. See *Study Shows Fathers Affect Daughters' Sex Lives*.

www.lifescript.com. This is a women's health informational Web site that provides easy access to hundreds of articles on women's psychosocial health issues. The Web site search facility yielded 110 articles for the search topic "fathers." Many of these are excellent, and references to original publications are provided. You can also sign up for the site's mailing list.

www.ppositivepath.net. This is a personal growth network with many articles relevant to father-daughter relationships. See especially M. Grose, *Fathers Raising Daughters*.

Nonfiction Works of Special Interest to the Daughters of Fathers in Specific Archetypes

For Daughters of Disapproving Fathers

Feeney, J., and Noller, P. *Adult Attachment*. Thousand Oaks, Calif.: Sage, 1996.

Robinson, M. *Longing for Daddy: Healing from the Pain of an Emotionally Distant Father*. New York: Doubleday, 2004.

Sperling, M. B., and Berman, M. B. *Attachment in Adults*. New York: Guilford Press, 1994.

For Daughters of Mentally Ill Fathers

Brown, E. M. *My Parents' Keeper: Adult Children of the Emotionally Disturbed*. Oakland, Calif.: New Harbinger, 1989.

Miller, S. *When Parents Have Problems: A Book for Teens and Older Children with an Abusive, Alcoholic, or Mentally Ill Parent*. Springfield, Ill.: Charles C. Thomas, 1995.

Ross, A. *Coping When a Parent Is Mentally Ill*. New York: Rosen Publishing Group, 2001.

Roth, K., Friedman, F., and Kreger, R. *Surviving a Borderline Parent: How to Heal Your Childhood Wounds and Build Trust, Boundaries, and Self-Esteem*. Oakland, Calif.: New Harbinger, 2003.

Secunda, V. *When Madness Comes Home: Help and Hope for the Children, Siblings, and Partners of the Mentally Ill*. New York: Hyperion, 1998.

Vine, P. *Families in Pain: Children, Siblings, Spouses, and Parents of the Mentally Ill Speak Out*. New York: Knopf Doubleday, 1982. An excellent volume.

For Daughters of Substance-Abusing Fathers

Barnard, M. (ed.). *Drug Addiction and Families*. Philadelphia: Jessica Kingsley, 2006.

Woititz, J. *Adult Children of Alcoholics*. Downers Grove, Ill.: Heath Communications, 1990. A classic, with lessons also relevant to adult children of other types of dysfunctional parents.

For Daughters of Abusive Fathers

Blume, E. S. *Secret Survivors: Uncovering Incest and Its Aftereffects in Women*. New York: Random House, 1990.

Gil, E. *Outgrowing the Pain: A Book for and About Adults Abused as Children*. New York: Dell, 1983.

Herman, J. L. *Father-Daughter Incest*. Cambridge, Mass.: Harvard University Press, 2000.

Rogriguez-Srednicki, O., and Twaite, J. A. *Understanding, Assessing, and Treating Adult Victims of Childhood Abuse*. New York: Jason Aronson, 2006.

Rosenbloom, D., and Williams, M. *Life After Trauma: A Workbook for Healing*. New York: Guilford Press, 1999.

For Daughters of Absent Fathers

Dunn, B. and Leonard, C. *Through a Season of Grief: Devotions for Your Journey from Mourning to Joy*. Nashville, Tenn.: Thomas Nelson, 2004.

Twaite, J. A., Silitsky, D., and Luchow, A. K. *Children of Divorce: Adjustment, Custody, Remarriage, and Recommendations for Clinicians*. Northvale, N.J.: Jason Aronson, 1998. Includes an excellent discussion of parental alienation syndrome and fathers who absent themselves to avoid conflict following divorce.

Web Sites and Support Groups for Daughters of Fathers in Specific Archetypes

www.aacap.org. The site of the American Academy of Child and Adolescent Psychiatry; many links to articles relevant to parental mental illness.

www.adultchildren.org. Resources for adult children of alcoholics.

www.alanon.alateen.org. Resources for children of alcoholics.

www.bipolar.about.com/b/. Specifically for children of parents with bipolar disorder.

www.psychcentral.com. Excellent resource for daughters of mentally ill fathers.

www.teenadvice.about.com/od/teenlifefaqsnadqas/a/mentalillness. Advice for teens with mentally ill parents.

www.wikihow/deal-with-a-drug-addicted-family-member. Resources for family members of substance abusers; see especially T. Brown and B. Rubenstein, *How to Deal with a Drug-Addicted Family Member or Loved One*.

Memoirs

Busby, C., and Busby, J. *The Year We Disappeared: A Father-Daughter Memoir*. New York: Bloomsbury, 2008.

Pryor, R. *Jokes My Father Never Told Me: Life, Love, and Loss with Richard Pryor*. New York: HarperCollins, 2006.

Vassel, R. *Daughters of Men: Portraits of African-American Women and Fathers*. New York: HarperCollins, 2007.

Fiction

Austin, J. *Emma*. New York: Penguin, 2003.

Bronte, C. *Jane Eyre*. New York: Penguin, 2006.

Burnett, F. *Little Princess*. Scotts Valley, Calif.: CreateSpace, 2009.

Cole, B. *My Father*. Bloomington, Ind.: Xlibris Corp., 2001.

Dickens, C. *A Tale of Two Cities*. Lyndhurst, N.J.: Barnes and Noble, 2004.

Eliot, G. *Middlemarch*. Lyndhurst, N.J.: Barnes and Noble, 2003.

Ephron, D. *Frannie in Pieces*. New York: HarperCollins, 2007.

Lamb, W. *I Know This Much Is True*. New York: HarperCollins, 2003.

Shelley, M. *Mathilda*. New York: Tark Classic Fiction, 2008.

Sparks, N. *The Last Song*. New York: Grand Central Publishing, 2009.
Shaw, R. *A Country Affair*. New York: Three Rivers Press, 2001.
Shephard, S. *The Visibles*. New York: Free Press, 2009.

Movies

Mike Cahill (director). (2007). *The King of California*.
Lee Daniels (director). (2009). *Precious*.
Laurence Dumore (director). (1997). *Father's Day*.
Victor Fleming (director). (1933). *Bombshell*.
Robert Greenwald (director). (1984). *The Burning Bed*.
Ruth Leitman (director). (1998). *Alma*.
Yasujiro Ozu (director). (1949). *Late Spring*.
Paul Shrader (director). (1999). *Affliction*.
Lee Tamahori (director). (1997). *Once Were Warriors*.

About the Author

Sarah Simms Rosenthal, who has a PhD in clinical social work from New York University, has a private practice in New York City treating individuals, couples, and families. She previously worked as an adolescent and family therapist at Phoenix House, a nonprofit substance abuse services agency, for fifteen years.

For more information, visit www.theunavailablefather.com.

Index

A

Abandonment response: death of father leading to, 106–110; following divorce of parents, 110–114

Absent Father Score, 136–137

Absent father stories: abandonment and idealized fantasy of, 105, 136–137; Anne's abandonment following divorce, 110–114, 118; Antonia's fantasy father, 106–110, 118; assessing the damage of, 136–137; Delphine's physically absent father, 114–118; path to recovery, 118–119

Abusive Father Score, 132–135

Abusive father stories: assessing damage done by, 123; assessing damage from, 132–135; extreme harm done to daughters, 69–70; Katie's physically abusive stepfather, 74–81; Margaret's intimacy issues from verbal abuse, 70–73; Michelle's sexual abuse by father, 81–86; path to recovery, 86–87

Abusive marriage/relationships: repeating childhood abuse through, 80–81; as response to problems with father, 43, 44–45. *See also* Childhood abuse

Adrienna's story, 13–17

ALANON, 53

ALATEEN, 53

Alcoholic fathers: assessing the damage of, 131–132; Carey's people-pleaser response to, 51–56, 66; Katherine's pain from, 56–60, 67

Alliance for the Mentally Ill, 47

American Psychiatric Association, 89

Anne's story, 110–114, 118

Antidepressants, 39

Antonia's story, 106–110, 118

Approval: failure of disapproving fathers to provide, 24–25; high achievement response seeking, 4–25, 50–51

Attachment disorder: disapproving fathers with, 3–25, 89; as response to verbal abuse, 73. *See also* Intimacy issues

Attention: promiscuity as cry for, 63, 65, 67, 87; substance abuse cry for, 63, 65, 67

Attitude substitution: assessing the impact on life by, 154–155; expanding your possibilities by, 148; modifying and refining new attitudes, 155–156; taking action for, 150–151; taking the time for, 152–153; thinking differently about yourself for, 149–150

Attitudes: assessing your childhood responses, 146–147; determining your development of, 143–145; identifying those you've carried into adulthood, 145–147; observe/read about other's to understand, 144–145; recognizing the ones limiting your happiness, 147–148; substituting new ones for ineffective, 148–153; talk to others about what you've learned about, 145

Auden, W. H., 97

B

Behavior substitution: assessing the impact on life by, 154–155; expanding

165